E

As a behavioral-health therapist, I spend many days trying to steer people away from the obtrusive, compulsive thinking that is destroying them, mentally, physically, and spiritually. Depression, anxiety, addiction, anger, fear, all of these negative emotions are often the result of the dark thoughts they entertain. Many times, maybe most times, I find myself reciting to them something I have learned from my friend, Eddie Turner. He is an absolute master at articulating both the difficulty in and the deliverance from the "stinking thinking" that many people have surrendered to. I have never been more excited to see a body of knowledge come to print. This book may very well put me out of business. I hope it does.

DR. MIKE COURTNEY, PH.D.
Founder and Director, Branches
Counseling Centers
Murfreesboro, Tennessee

From the moment I was told about this book, I knew that Eddie Turner and I had walked a different but similar path. Three months after my supernatural deliverance from depression and suicide many years ago, I began the process of taking control of my thoughts. Even though I had never heard teaching on renewing the mind or pulling down strongholds, the Holy Spirit opened the eyes of my understanding. I began to live in the pages of the Bible. The three passages of scripture that kept me awake many nights were 1 John 4:4, Galatians 2:20, and 2 Corinthians 5:21. My tormenting days of believing that I was losing my mind were transformed into days of unspeakable joy and peace. Talk about "laboring to enter into the rest," I did—day and night—night and day. Today, I will tell you it was by the grace of God that I determined to persuade my mind that what God said about me was true! You are the righteousness of God in Christ Jesus! Yes...you! You are the only one who can choose to believe or reject the thoughts that bombard your mind. Apply the teachings in this book as Eddie shares his testimony, scriptures, and the "how-to's" of taking charge of your thoughts. You have the power to choose a victim mentality or a triumphant victor's mentality. You personally choose life or death for you. Eddie's testimony, the scriptures he shares, and his instructions are tools that will change your life—if you apply them!

GERMAINE COPELAND
Author of the bestselling *Prayers
That Avail Much*® book series

Years ago, I met a pastor who would prove out to be a divine connection, a lifetime friend, and a frequent voice into my life. Pastor Eddie Turner is one of the most gifted and faithful pastors I've ever met. His story of being set free from torment in his mind is a message so needed in the body of Christ in these times. We've ministered to the spirit and the body, but still many are held captive in their souls. Pastor Eddie has a gift from heaven to minister to those individuals. What he has learned from God's Word, experienced in his life, and now has written in the pages of this book, I believe will help to change the lives of multitudes who have previously been locked in darkness. Thank you, Pastor Eddie! You're one of my very closest friends and my hero.

MARK BRAZEE
Lead Pastor, World Outreach Church of Tulsa
Tulsa, Oklahoma

Eddie Turner has taken his life experiences and knowledge of scripture to help the readers truly find freedom—"no condemnation" type freedom that the apostle Paul says is promised to those in Christ. This book can arm you to win the battle for your mind.

DOUG CLAY
General Superintendent of the Assemblies of God
Springfield, Missouri

There are few books that will grab and hold your attention as does Eddie Turner's, *Conquering the Chaos in Your Mind*. What makes this work so powerful is the sheer honesty and personal nature of Eddie's struggle, journey, and victory, AND the powerful application of God's Word and the mighty working of the Holy Spirit in his life. Though some may have never experienced the depth of Eddie's battle, countless people will identify with it. Those who have known tormenting fear and paralyzing anxiety will greatly benefit from Eddie's powerful testimony, and the principles he shares will help every believer who needs to know how to overcome attacks of darkness, even if they are "the little foxes that spoil the vines." I greatly appreciate Eddie sharing both his heart and these dynamic tools that bring liberty to those who are bound.

TONY COOKE
Bible teacher and author
Tulsa, Oklahoma

The truths that set Pastor Eddie free from mental torment are powerfully communicated in this fantastic book through his own personal testimony. As you read, it's as if you live through this experience with him and learn what he learned. His teaching on this subject is some of the best I have ever found and has brought freedom and deliverance to many people. I know this book will do the same for many, many more.

GREG FRITZ
Greg Fritz Ministries
Tulsa, Oklahoma

CONQUERING
THE CHAOS IN
YOUR MIND

CONQUERING
THE CHAOS IN
YOUR MIND

FINDING FREEDOM FROM TORMENTING & ANXIOUS THOUGHTS

EDDIE TURNER

Published by Harrison House Publishers
Shippensburg, PA 17257

Cover design by Eileen Rockwell
Interior design by Terry Clifton

ISBN 13 TP: 978-1-6803-1576-9
ISBN 13 eBook: 978-1-6803-1577-6
ISBN 13 HC: 978-1-6803-1579-0
ISBN 13 LP: 978-1-6803-1578-3

For Worldwide Distribution, Printed in the U.S.A.
3 4 5 6 7 8 / 25 24 23 22 21

DEDICATION

I lovingly dedicate this book to my high school sweetheart, my bride, and my best friend, Amanda. Though I write about my experiences, she patiently walked through each of these experiences with me. Her constant encouragement and unwavering faith has been my model and inspiration for over forty years.

I would also like to thank my friend and editor, Kaye Mountz. She heard my story and urged me repeatedly to put it in print. Her guiding hand and professional insight has been invaluable to me on this project.

Finally, I dedicate this book to all the silent sufferers of mental anguish and anxiety who fight the overwhelming mental and emotional darkness that seems to never permanently leave. I pray as you read my story, you gain hope and insight to start truly believing that you can enjoy daily peace.

CONTENTS

FOREWORD

I DO "FUNNY" FOR A LIVING. IT'S NOT ALWAYS EASY. BUT I HAVE BEEN A comedian for over 25 years and well, some would say I have been pretty successful at it. One of the greatest challenges for any comedian is to get an audience to laugh when the comedian is not feeling very funny. To be honest, I've been pretty good at that too. And like many comedians, I have used my jokes to mask the pain that I really felt inside—the sounds playing inside my head. *"You're not good enough." "You will never amount to anything." "If they really knew you they would never love you."*

Comedian or not, most of us have, at one time or another, fought the battle for our mind. Our family history, the poor choices we made, the pressure of the world around us, even the lessons we learned in Sunday school, all run together to make this "demonic" playlist that wants to dominate and dictate all the other thoughts that we have. Many of us try to outrun it. We think if we can be busy enough, earn enough, have fun enough, drink enough, we will stay ahead of the soundtrack and at the very least, ignore the voices most of the time. The problem is, the faster we go, the louder the tape plays.

Others put up a good fight with the feeble weapons they know about. They get a diagnosis. They enroll in lifetime counseling. And they load up with a ton of prescriptions. Now, I'm not against that. My brother and I actually started a counseling center that sees nearly 2,000 people every month. I have my shrink on speed dial. And my pharmacist knows me by first name. God has given us wonderful mental health professionals to meet us in those dark times, talk us off the ledge, and get us back out on the stage. Frankly, counseling and 75 milligrams of Effexor has made the woman I am today. Whatever you have to do to fight the tape, do it.

But what if there is another way? A divine addition that lowers the dose, makes the counseling more effective. Pulls out root of the weeds in your mind that were watered by those nagging voices. What if God, in His infinite wisdom, placed in His Word our salvation and our solution for this battle we fight. What if it is really true that "our struggle is not against flesh and blood, but against the rulers, against the authorities, against the powers of this dark world and against the spiritual forces of evil in the heavenly realms?" And what if God wants to equip us with everything we need, not only to survive this fight in our head but to "conquer the chaos" and live the abundant, joyful life that He promises us we can live?

Listen to this, that is exactly what God wants to do and in fact, has done. Pastor Eddie Turner is absolutely a master on this subject. His messages have helped thousands, including me, to overcome voices in our heads, turn off the soundtrack of Satan, and once and for all find the "peace that passes all understanding." His teaching is practical, personal, and powerful. He tells you what's going on, what has to be done, and who you can count on. I am so excited about this book. I have watched the destruction that comes from losing this battle and I have lived with the consequences in my own life. No more. This message, this book will help so many, including me, fight the good fight, live the blessed life, and win the war in Jesus' name, and that is no joke.

CHONDA PIERCE
Christian Comedian, Dove Award Winner
Board of Directors, Branches Counseling Center

INTRODUCTION

WITH HIS LITTLE HANDS CLUTCHED AGAINST THE SIDE OF HIS HEAD, the eleven-year-old looked at me in desperation and said, "I can't get these thoughts out of my head." My heart broke as I glanced over at his parents sitting huddled up together weeping for their innocent, cherished son.

"Sir, I have driven over four hundred miles to see you. I heard about what you went through and how you are free. Can you help me? I have lost my wife and career because I can't shut my mind off," were the words of the forty-five-year-old businessman sitting in my office.

Story after story reveal many of the same scenes and much of the same pain: racing thoughts, crippling anxiety, paralyzing fear, and a mind that simply will not turn off. With each story I have heard, I reflect on the day I laid emotionally broken on the floor of my den.

I was convinced my life was over. Fear and paranoia had taken me prisoner, and hopeless anxiety rolled over me like a crashing wave. I felt like my head was about to explode.

5

As I lay there crying with my face buried in the carpet, thoughts relentlessly bombarded my mind. *You are going crazy! You are losing your mind. They are coming to take you to a mental hospital. You'll be locked up. Your family members had to go to insane asylums. You are next.*

In total desperation, I screamed out, "Oh, Lord Jesus, You've got to come help me!"

Suddenly, I sensed someone was in the room. I raised up quickly expecting to see my neighbor, but instead, I was looking into the face of Jesus.

"Eddie, what would you have Me do for you?" were His first words to me.

Over the next few minutes, Jesus talked to me about the thought life and taught me how to take control of my mind. He changed my life!

I'll share more of what He said in upcoming chapters, but I'm forever grateful that on that day Jesus set me on the path of freedom from depression, anxiety, and a mind paralyzed by paranoia.

Although that visitation from Jesus started my journey toward mental freedom, during the next few months, I still had good days and bad days. Some days I could bring my mind to a place of peace, but other days it was difficult to concentrate and stay focused. I continued to battle oppressive and tormenting thoughts.

One particular Wednesday was one of those days. My mind was tired, and emotionally I was drained. I was trying to study for a Wednesday evening Bible study but concentrating was tough. Being weary, I finally pushed back from my desk and just sat down on the floor. In hushed tones I began to just repeat the name of Jesus. As soon as I did, I felt myself lifting up. At first, I almost felt dizzy. Then suddenly, I realized I was going up, and the next thing I knew I was standing in heaven, and Jesus was standing in front of me. The things He told me and the things I saw became the inspiration and motivation for this book.

From that day forward, I have been on a quest to help others get mentally and emotionally free. I want to share how *you can* conquer the chaos and live in peace! *You can* win the battle for your mind and never allow a stronghold of fear, unforgiveness, lust, or anxiety to control your life again.

In the chapters that follow, I will teach you how powerful a single thought can be and how you can control your thought life. Using dozens of Bible verses and telling numerous personal stories, you will learn how to take back your most prized possession—*your mind*.

EDDIE TURNER

Chapter 1

'YOU MUST HAVE A DEMON'

EARLY NOVEMBER 1986, I WAS DRIVING IN THE TOWN WHERE I HAD been pastoring for three years. Over thirty years later, I don't remember where I was going, but I remember the moment during that drive that sent my life in a downward spiral for the next two years.

There was nothing in particular on my mind causing me to be worried or concerned. In fact, a few months earlier, our small church had seen an infusion of about thirty people, and we were getting close to the one hundred mark in attendance. As a twenty-eight-year-old pastor who had been raised in a small family church of forty or fifty members, the thought of leading a church with one hundred in Sunday attendance was a dream come true.

Our little town of Algood, Tennessee, only had 2,000 people. The district superintendent of our church

9

organization encouraged my wife, Amanda, and me to give the little church a try. On a good Sunday in 1983, the congregation had forty attendees including adults and children. He told us it would be a good first pastorate, and if it didn't work out, not to worry because they were thinking of closing the little church due to its overwhelming financial struggles.

The church was in a tough position financially. They had launched out and built a sanctuary that would seat two hundred people with related facilities—bathrooms and a few small classrooms. The monthly mortgage was $1,347, which included an interest rate of 11.75%. So, with a total income of less than $28,000 a year, every penny was stretched as far as it could go. Between the mortgage payment, building insurance, utility bills, cleaning supplies, and Sunday school materials for our two children's classes, there wasn't any money left over at the end of the month. The church family was doing all they could, but the congregation was composed of a few young couples and a few retired couples. So financial resources were thin.

Amanda likes to tell people that the day she was able to add hamburger to our "Hamburger Helper" was the moment breakthrough occurred for us. Those early years were a walk of faith. Growing up in a small Pentecostal church with limited resources, it never occurred to me that this was a sacrifice. I assumed this was the normal price of ministry.

But on that November day, things were actually improving. Amanda had landed a good job in the accounting department of a local company which provided health insurance for our family. And the greatest thing was that our ten-month-old firstborn had graduated from crawling to standing. It was a good season in our lives!

Yet as I drove down the road that afternoon, a strange and unsettling thought darted into my mind. It seemed like it came out of nowhere. Over the years during my youth, I had often found myself allowing my mind to wander. I would daydream about being a sports hero, girls, fun times for the upcoming weekend, girls, hitting a homerun in the bottom of the ninth inning to win the game for my high school baseball team, girls, or scoring the game-winning touchdown. Even as an adult, I would daydream about vacations, my future, maybe one day pastoring a big church, and an assortment of hopes and aspirations for my family.

I also struggled with lustful thoughts and a desire to view pornography during my adolescent and early adult years. I never talked about it because of shame and embarrassment, so I just repented continually and prayed sincerely every day that God would supernaturally deliver me from this secret prison. Being a pastor and struggling with lustful thoughts was a huge taboo. Unfortunately like many other ministers, I lived alone in my private hell of condemnation and mental torment.

But that particular day as I drove down the road, my mind was not wandering. I was not daydreaming. Yet suddenly and without warning, a vicious and hideous thought pierced my mind like a sharp dagger: *You must be demon possessed!*

Where did that come from? I wondered. I still remember the sting of the accusation that accompanied the thought.

Immediately, I thought to myself, *That is the craziest thing I have ever heard.* I shook my head, chuckled, and kept driving down the road.

A couple of days later, I read in the local paper about a neighboring church having a huge outreach event. In fact, the church was the largest church in our area, and all the important people in town went there. I felt a cringe of jealousy as I read the article, realizing this church had the people and resources to make community impact and our little church didn't. I knew I shouldn't have those feelings and immediately asked the Lord to bless their efforts and forgive me for thinking that way.

> Suddenly and without warning, a vicious and hideous thought pierced my mind like a sharp dagger: *You must be demon possessed!*

Right on the heels of that simple, little prayer, that same thought invaded again: *You must be demon possessed.*

Again, that horrible rogue thought stung me like a wasp or spider. This time, it lingered in my mind longer than just a moment. In fact, I found myself answering the thought, "I am not demon possessed! Christians are not demon possessed! I am a pastor! This is crazy!" Within a few moments, I became distracted again, and my thoughts drifted to another subject.

Over the next few weeks, time and time again, I was confronted with pastors and church members of other churches telling me wonderful reports and all the great things happening in their churches. As they talked, I tried to share in their excitement, but each time as I walked away, thoughts of rejection and heaviness filled my mind. I even had feelings of anger toward those people for "rubbing it in" because I knew our little church wasn't doing those things.

In the days that followed, every time I would begin to pray, anxious and tormenting thoughts became more prevalent: *There's no need to pray. You are demon possessed. You know you are. Demon-possessed people think bad things about pastors and churches. God doesn't love you, or your church would be doing better. God can't bless a church with a pastor who is demon possessed. That's the reason your church isn't growing. How can you think such awful things?*

Lustful thoughts invaded my mind as well and were followed by thoughts of persecution and condemnation: *See there, you are demon possessed or you wouldn't think those ugly things. Christians don't think things like that. Pastors especially don't think things like that. You're no good. God cannot possibly love you.*

Little by little, the tormenting thoughts became more consuming. Instead of an occasional stinging thought out of nowhere, the harassing thoughts started filling my mind at random times during the day and grew with intensity.

At first, I laughed off the thoughts, kicked out the thoughts, or focused my mind on something else. But over time, as the tormenting thoughts continued, I found myself feeling more and more convinced that these thoughts must be true or I wouldn't be thinking them. As time passed, the thoughts were getting more difficult to erase and remove from my mind. They lingered longer, and my excuses for them being in my mind started fading.

Over the years, I have been asked dozens of times, "Why would you think something that ridiculous? Didn't you know better?"

Let me answer that question with a question: Why do you think some of the ridiculous things you think? Why do we all entertain thoughts that are obviously not true?

Unfortunately, the truth is, too many of us believe lies about ourselves.

The intelligent, young man who lives in fear that he will never succeed in class, yet his grades always prove differently. Where did his fearful thoughts originate from? The beautiful young lady who thinks nobody desires her because she views herself less than attractive. Where did she get those thoughts? The person who lives in a prison of insecurity held captive by thoughts of inferiority, yet everyone associated with him or her sees wonderful talents and abilities. How did that person form such a negative opinion? Or have you seen someone you don't even know or someone you've never met but accusatory thoughts about him or her flood your mind?

Why do any of us think the ridiculous things we think? Didn't I know better? The answer is yes and no. Yes, I knew deep in my heart that I wasn't demon possessed, but the continual harassing thoughts were chipping away at my confidence. And no, there were things I did not know about taking control of my thoughts and prohibiting Satan's accusatory darts from invading my mind. I soon discovered the truthfulness of Hosea 4:6, which says, "My people are destroyed for lack of knowledge."

I also soon confided in my wife. At first, she just laughed and said, "Eddie, that's silly! Don't think that way!" But soon, she realized those persistent, tormenting thoughts were starting to adversely affect me. She watched as I would sit and stare as in a trance, never answering her questions because I was paralyzed by tormenting thoughts.

Amanda reassured me that none of those accusatory things I was thinking were true. She reminded me constantly that I was a godly and sincere man, our church was growing, people's lives were being changed, new families were coming, and so many prayers had been answered. She would grab my hands and pray with me, and I would sense a temporary relief. But over time, even her affirming words were drowned by the continual onslaught of harassing, tormenting thoughts: *You are demon possessed. You have never been saved. You are a fake. Christians do not think the thoughts you think.*

After a few months of the continual onslaught of these accusations, I finally came to the place where I couldn't sleep. Amanda encouraged me to make an appointment to see my spiritual overseers. She said they understood the stress of ministry, and surely, they could help me. So, I told them about the tormenting thoughts, my inability to concentrate, and not being able to sleep. I told them how the thoughts were relentless, and I was starting to struggle with fear. And I told them how more and more I did not want to be around people. They kindly listened and shared a couple of scriptures with me, and they suggested I take a week off and get some rest.

I did as they advised and took a few days off, but my mind never turned off. I got away from the church and the responsibilities, but I soon discovered the church and responsibilities were not my struggle. The harassing thoughts continued even though I was several hundred miles away.

Now some thirty years later, I help and coach pastors weekly who are fighting mental wars in their minds. They often tell me, "If I could just get some time off, I think I will be okay." Certainly, quality time off is good! It enables pastors to get away from the heavy loads and unending responsibilities we often carry. The stress of knowing that every phone call, text, or email could be a crisis, an unhappy parishioner, or a church problem can weigh heavily on our minds and emotions.

In fact, no matter what sort of job you work—whether you're a stay-at-home mom, busy in a thriving career, retired from it, or a student on the path to your professional future—life can still bring heavy burdens and responsibilities to bear. Stress does not discriminate!

Removing oneself from a stressful environment for a season is healthy and provides an opportunity for mental, emotional, and physical rest. But if the mental and emotional stress is caused by unhealthy thinking or a satanic attack, simply changing locations will not solve the problem.

Friends and family members lovingly said to me, "Just think about something else! Don't think about it! Get your mind on another subject. Get busy doing something." Oh, how I wish it would have been that easy and simple. I was losing control of my mind, and I was unable to think about the things I wanted to think about or should think about.

By the end of January 1987, I was in real trouble. I didn't sleep over three hours at a time. I hated the nights. During the day there was someone to talk to, something to do which kept my mind partially occupied, but at night I was alone with those tormenting thoughts.

Tossing and turning, up and down was my nightly routine. Late at night, I would get so tired and drift off to sleep in my recliner, only to be startled awake by a tormenting dream. Once awake, the harassing thoughts ensued again. Though I tried and tried, I couldn't turn my mind off. I couldn't stop the harassing, tormenting thoughts. Fearful, negative, impure, heavy, dark oppressive thoughts bombarded my mind continually while I was awake, and those same thoughts were keeping me from resting at night.

With the precision of a military machine gun, accusatory, condemning, and painful thoughts fired into my mind, over and over and over. Relentless, unending, continual accusations invaded my mind like a tsunami sweeping away every fiber of joy and faith I possessed.

Finally, I was so full of fear I wouldn't leave my house. Fear had bullied me for so long I was convinced if I left my house, people would see the demons on me. People would be fearful of me and run away.

> With the precision of a military machine gun, accusatory, condemning, and painful thoughts fired into my mind, over and over and over.

These anxious thoughts did not continue their onslaught on my mind only but began showing up in my body as well. I was experiencing multiple physical symptoms: tightness in my chest, nausea, and what felt like a vise grip locked around my head. Even my eyesight was literally becoming dim. I would turn every light on in the house because the house always seemed dark. I began to lose my memory and couldn't remember people's names. I cried so much that I lived with a constant headache. Amanda took me to three different physicians, but they couldn't find anything physically wrong.

By this time, the few tormenting thoughts had turned into an avalanche of every negative and fearful thought imaginable: *You are losing your mind. You are going crazy. Demon-possessed people lose their minds. They are coming to get you at any time to take you away to a mental hospital. You belong in a mental hospital with other demon-possessed people. You will never see your son grow up. Your grandmother was in a mental hospital, and that is where you will end up. Don't touch anyone because the demon in you will get on them. You are not a pastor; you have been a phony all along. The devil orchestrated you being at this church to destroy it. You might even be the Antichrist. Somewhere along the way, you committed the unpardonable sin. Your wife is going to leave you. You are weak. It's never going to get better. You are demon possessed. You are an embarrassment to your family. No one will listen to you when you preach. You're too messed up. Just go ahead and end your life so your wife and son can live in peace.*

Over and over, the suggestions and thoughts of ending my life played out in my mind. Hopelessness and darkness shrouded my thoughts and countenance. I didn't want to live this way for the rest of my life, so what was the use in living at all? It seemed that no one understood what I was going through, and I was causing my wife misery. Eventually, the church people would get weary with a pastor who was struggling rather than one who was healthy spiritually.

During this time, a friend gave me a book by Kenneth E. Hagin titled *What to do When Faith Seems Weak and Victory Lost.* Being raised in a traditional Pentecostal church, I had been warned to stay away from all those "so-called faith guys." Yet, out of desperation and desiring peace of mind, I threw caution to the wind and started reading the book. As I read, to my amazement, I would get temporary relief and peace in my mind. I read the book from cover to cover multiple times. As soon as I finished reading it, I would start back over reading again. As I read, my mind became quiet, the harassing thoughts ceased, and I enjoyed a temporary peace.

Rev. Hagin said something which served as my hope and my light when everything else seemed to be so dark. In chapter four, titled "Be Sure No Doubt or Unbelief is Permitted in Your Life," he writes:

> Thoughts may come and persist in staying. But thoughts that are not put into word or action die unborn. Remember this also. The most holy saints of God have found, at times, thoughts in their mind that their heart resented.[1]

For the first time, I found someone who reassured me that I was not the only person who had encountered harassing thoughts. His words brought a glimmer of hope that I was not demon possessed for having these ugly, terrible thoughts. I repeated his word to myself often: "The most holy saints of God have found, at times, thoughts in their mind that their heart resented."

In my excitement to find help, I mentioned the book to folks in my church organization. They rebuked me, warning, "He's way out there! Stay away from him!" But like a drowning man grabbing for any help available, I kept reading. A few minister friends called me during this same time and warned me that our organization would not look kindly on me if I became one of those "faith guys." They got to me too late; the book was helping me.

The only time I could slow the onslaught of tormenting thoughts was when I was reading that book and my Bible. But, unfortunately, I couldn't read twenty-four hours a day. So, as soon as I set the book down or ceased praying, the mental torment ensued.

By the middle of February 1987, I only left my house for church on Sunday and Wednesday. I would go to church and preach, and remarkably, people would come and enjoy the services. We even had people's lives being changed during that time. But as soon as the service was over, I would run to my office and refuse to shake hands with anyone because I didn't want the demon in me to get on the church family. Amanda would greet all the people each Sunday and kindly make excuses for me. Then once everyone had left, she would retrieve me from my office and drive me home.

To this very day, Amanda recalls exciting moments in our young son's life—his first steps, first birthday party, and first words—but I don't remember them. My mind was paralyzed. I was bound and broken.

Why was this happening to me? After all, I was raised in a good home with wonderful parents. We all went to church every Sunday and Wednesday. My grandfather was the pastor of our church, and my grandmother oversaw the women's ministry. My dad was an usher, and my mother was the church organist.

Since I was ten years old, I aspired to be like my grandfather and pastor a congregation. I was always healthy. I had never been in trouble. I was the first in my family to graduate from college. I married my beautiful high school sweetheart and was excited about being in the ministry, helping people, and raising a family.

But in 1987 I found myself messed up, thinking I was losing my mind, going crazy, and demon possessed. By day, I was a prisoner in our little house, and by night, I was paralyzed with tormenting thoughts. I was unable to concentrate, unable to work, unable to eat, and unable to sleep. I couldn't tell my friends in the church what I was experiencing for fear that they might leave the church. Seriously now, who wants to attend a church where the pastor is demon possessed and going crazy? I couldn't tell my ministry peers of the struggle because they might tell the church officials who would dismiss me as pastor.

I had a grandmother and other family members who had spent time in a mental hospital before they died. In those years, health care for the mentally ill and emotionally challenged was not as helpful as it is today. I had dreams and nightmares of being admitted to such a place against my will, and I would imagine my little boy waving at me through the metal bars just like I waved goodbye to my grandmother many years earlier.

All hope seemed lost, my ministry was over, and I was losing my mind. I was convinced I would soon lose my family and my freedom. Then one Saturday in February 1987, *everything changed.*

Questions:

❶. What are some tormenting thoughts that have harassed your life?

❷. How did you respond to the harassing thoughts?

❸. What lies have you or someone you love believed about yourselves?

Prayer:

Heavenly Father, according to Your Word in 2 Timothy 1:7, I have been promised a sound mind, free from worry and anxiety. I ask You to enable me to guard my thought life and learn to prevent Satan access to my mind. I declare that I have the mind of Christ, a thought life of peace and joy. In Jesus' name, amen.

Chapter 2

JESUS APPEARED TO ME

AMANDA HAD BEEN ASKING DAILY IF I WOULD ACCOMPANY HER AND our toddler to eat breakfast and grocery shop on an upcoming Saturday morning. Since I was no longer leaving the house, she understood I needed a lot of encouragement to venture out.

Reluctantly, I agreed to join them and spent the next few days psyching myself up to leave the house. I quoted scriptures on overcoming fear and continually read my Bible and prayed, but the tormenting thoughts seemed to swell even louder and more exaggerated: *As soon as people see you in the restaurant, they will know you are crazy. You are an embarrassment to your family. The demon in you will manifest in public. Worse yet, the police will be called. You need to stay in your house where everyone will be safe from you. You are demon possessed and losing your mind!*

Saturday morning arrived, and we gathered enough toys to keep our toddler entertained for a few hours before heading to a local restaurant. The restaurant was full of people laughing and talking. We were seated, and our breakfast was ordered. I was doing okay until, without warning, an avalanche unleashed. A wave of negative thoughts began pounding my mind: *Look around! These people know about you. They know you are demon possessed. You are losing your mind. Get out of here! The demon will get on your waitress. You are going crazy.*

Over and over, the thoughts raced into my mind, firing at me so fast I seemed powerless to resist or put up a fight to stop them. I started physically shaking my head and rubbing my forehead to stop the thoughts. But to no avail, the harassment continued.

Within minutes, I felt like the room was closing in on me. Sweating profusely, my head was pounding, and the noise level seemed to intensify. Amanda knew something was wrong and asked if I was okay. I told her I needed to leave.

"Please stay! It will be okay," she said squeezing my hand.

I tried to fight through, but I couldn't take it. I had to get out of there. I quickly jumped up and rushed out of the restaurant, running to the car.

Tears poured down my cheeks as I realized the thoughts were true: *I am losing my mind. They're going to put me away. I will never be able to go out in public again. I will die in a mental hospital. I can't get this demon out of mind. I will end up in hell. I don't want to go to hell. I am*

going to lose everything—my family, my house, my church.
Everything will be gone because I am crazy.

A few minutes later, Amanda and our toddler came to
the car—both of them in tears. I told her to get me home.
Neither of us will ever forget that drive home in silence.
My mind was racing uncontrollably, and I seemed powerless to do anything but listen to all the negative, accusatory
thoughts and images flooding my mind.

As we pulled into our driveway, Amanda told me we
needed groceries, and she would take our son on to the
store with her.

"Okay," I said, quietly walking into the house feeling
every bit a man defeated. Stumbling into our den, I fell face
first into the carpet, weeping uncontrollably.

In anguish I screamed out, "Oh, Lord, I am truly losing
my mind. What happened to me? How did I get this way?
I am dying. Please, Lord Jesus, come and help me."

Hopelessness and helplessness overwhelmed my heart
and mind. I knew somehow this was the end. I realized I
was not going to get well; I did not know how to get well.
I could not even explain how this whole mental and emotional ordeal had started or how I had spiraled to such
depths of complete defeat and despair.

In desperation I screamed again, "Lord Jesus, I am
dying. Please come help me."

I don't know how long I laid with my face buried in the
carpet, but eventually I stopped crying and became quiet.

Suddenly, I sensed something unusual. It was at that moment, I realized I was no longer in the room alone.

As I raised my head, I saw a man's feet, and on the feet were sandals. At first, I thought my neighbor must have seen me come home and came to check on me. So, I quickly raised up on my hands and knees, not wanting him to see me in such a broken position.

To my utter amazement, standing in front of me was Jesus. He wore a white robe, and His hair was long, touching His shoulders. His facial features resembled the renderings we often see in pictures and paintings.

His presence left me in awe.

Immediately, fear and anxiety which had been my constant companion for months were gone. A calming sense of peace overwhelmed and quieted the tormenting thoughts that plagued me.

It was as if the entire world stood still.

Different types of thoughts now flooded my mind: *Was this real? Had I died and gone to heaven? Was I hallucinating? Was this a dream?*

Pausing to look around the room, I realized to my surprise I was still in my den. I didn't say a word—I couldn't. Jesus was still standing in front of me. I leaned back on my knees without taking my eyes off Him.

I don't know how long we looked at each other, but I remember His sweet smile.

"Eddie, what would you have Me do for you?" He asked.

Quickly, I replied, "Lord Jesus, these thoughts are killing me."

Jesus smiled and said, "I told you thoughts are as vapors, smoke."

Immediately, my mind went back months earlier to a prayer time right after this tormenting ordeal began. In prayer, I had asked the Lord why I was having these crazy thoughts, and a strong impression of the words *vapors, smoke* rose up from my spirit inside me. Being young in walking in the Spirit, I didn't pay it any attention because it didn't make any sense to me.

Yet on this day, I realized the Spirit of God told me months earlier that the deception of Satan's attack is nothing more than a smoke screen—without strength and power. His arsenal is empty lies.

A few years later, I read another book by Kenneth E. Hagin titled *The Believer's Authority.* In that book, he detailed a vision in which an evil spirit resembling a little monkey ran between Jesus and himself. This evil spirit spread out something that looked like a smoke screen or dark cloud. This evil spirit was trying to prohibit Rev. Hagin from seeing and receiving from the Lord.[2]

> The deception of Satan's attack is nothing more than a smoke screen—without strength and power.

In retrospect, those months I lived in anguish, I had God's Word on the subject. The Lord had faithfully and early on revealed to me the truth about those tormenting thoughts, but I didn't pick up on it. The answer He gave me was a subtle impression that came in prayer, but I was listening and looking for something more dramatic and spectacular.

Since that day, I have learned to listen for the *subtle word* from the Lord, the *still small voice* as mentioned in 1 Kings 19:12. The visions, dreams, and spectacular events from God are wonderful and dynamic, but they are usually the exception and not the rule. In fact, my spectacular visitations only occurred when I was in real trouble. If I had taken heed to the subtle word of the Lord earlier—when He first spoke to me—I would have saved myself much heartache and torment.

Since I have learned this principle of how the Spirit normally works and guides, I don't seek visions or spectacular manifestations. I am satisfied when I get my answer from my daily devotions, sense the inward witness of the Holy Spirit (Romans 8:14, Proverbs 20:27), or hear the still small voice (1 Kings 19:11-13).

As soon as Jesus said, "I told you thoughts are as vapors, smoke," He reached down and touched the right side of my head and began pulling out of my head what appeared to be a banner with writing on it.

The only way I can describe the banner is to say it was similar to a huge banner you would see stretched across the road announcing some special event in a city or town. Once Jesus pulled it out completely, I could see the writing on it which said, "You are demon possessed."

That was the main tormenting thought which had started the entire nightmare. That was the thought that popped into my mind several months earlier while I was driving down the road. That was the recurring thought that tormented me continually that I could not turn off or find a response to stop it. That was the evil thought that was driving me crazy.

To my amazement, Jesus blew on the banner, and it disappeared like a vapor of smoke.

Over the years, as I have replayed this scene many times, I realize Jesus did not try to logically reason away the thought. Neither did He spend any time answering the accusation. Jesus simply destroyed it.

One of Satan's most effective schemes is seducing us into a mental question-and-answer game in our minds. I discovered that every time I mentally came up with a logical answer, Satan would always come back with another question; the game never stopped. I found myself on the defensive and eventually unable to adequately satisfy all the questions that produced doubt and fear. If Satan can keep us in the arena of logical thought, he will defeat us every time.

> If Satan can keep us in the arena of logical thought, he will defeat us every time.

Then without saying a word, Jesus reached down again and touched the right side of my head and pulled out another banner. As He pulled it out, I could see writing on it that said, "God doesn't love you."

This was the other thought that tormented me over and over, day and night. By that point, I was convinced I was beyond the love of God because of the harassing and evil thoughts flooding my mind. I remember thinking that I must be beyond the love of God or these thoughts would cease. I had never heard anyone in ministry share this type of experience, and I knew God loved ministers. So I concluded that if I was experiencing such torment, then God must not love me. But what had I done to cause Him not to love me? This was the thought process that invaded my mind daily and wrestled with me continually.

Jesus never answered the question of why this was happening to me. Neither did He give me a revelation on how to logically respond to the tormenting thoughts. Jesus simply destroyed the thought.

Once again, without saying a word, Jesus blew on the banner with the writing on it, and it evaporated like a puff of smoke. I sat on my knees in total silence.

It was as if I were somewhere else, but I realized I was kneeling in my den. I remember Jesus was not in a hurry, and He smiled often at me. With each smile came an overwhelming sense of peace and love that I had never before experienced.

A third time, Jesus reached down and pulled out another white banner out of the side of my head. To my amazement this banner had no writing on it but was totally blank. Instead of blowing on it, as He had done the other two banners, He wadded it up into a paper ball.

As I watched this scene unfold, Jesus then said, "Eddie, there's your problem!" pointing to the corner of the room.

There in the corner of my den, I saw two hairy looking creatures that appeared to be the size of monkeys. I couldn't really tell how tall they were because they were huddled together in the corner hiding and cowering in fear.

Jesus looked back at me and then looked away toward the monkey creatures again. He did this a couple of times. Each time He looked at them, they would quake in fear. I could see the hair all over their bodies shaking. When Jesus looked at me, peace flooded me, but when He looked at them, they violently trembled in fear.

Without saying anything else, Jesus threw the wadded-up banner toward the two monkey-looking creatures. When He did, they screeched a horrible scream and grabbed each other. I watched them for a few moments. They shook and whimpered with their heads buried in the corner of the room, refusing to look at Jesus.

The whole time this scene played out, I never experienced any fear. Even though I was in the presence of demon spirits, I never felt anxious or nervous. The presence of Jesus completely drove out the fear. Isn't that what the Word of God says, "There is no fear in love; but perfect love casts out fear..." (1 John 4:18).

It was apparent the two demon spirits were experiencing a lot of fear. I have purposely remembered that scene many times during the years when fear tries to invade me. I remember it was the devil's imps which were afraid—not Jesus or myself.

After a few moments, I looked back at Jesus, and once again He smiled at me. Then instantly, He was gone. I didn't see Him ascend or even slowly disappear. He just was gone. I quickly glanced to the corner where the monkey creatures were, and they also were gone.

I don't know how long I sat on the floor after this occurred. I remember sitting there simply weeping. I wasn't weeping as I had for the past several months due to fear and torment but because of the incredible peace and rest I was experiencing in my mind.

Sometime later, Amanda and our toddler returned home. She walked into the den and found me crying. She asked if I was okay. I shook my head yes, but I could not talk. I tried to tell her what had happened, but all I could do was cry. For the next three days, I cried continually, but it was not a cry of anguish. I was completely enveloped in an overwhelming sense of peace, rest, and comfort. I was unable to put sentences together without crying. The next few nights, I slept like a baby and only woke a couple of times during the night. When I did wake up, there was no fear or anxiety, and I was able to drift back off to sleep.

During the next few days, I remained in my house, but it was no longer because of fear. Jesus' presence remained on me. It was as if a blanket of peace, comfort, and rest covered me. I didn't really understand what it was, but I didn't want to lose it. My mind was at rest. Tormenting thoughts ceased. The nagging feeling of fear was gone. Chaos was silent. The headaches went away, the constant nausea disappeared, and I didn't feel the tightening vise grip around my head any longer. I even started noticing little things, like the weather, beautiful smells, and the fun behavior of my toddler.

Although I didn't talk a lot to Amanda, I was once again "present" with her, not just existing in the same room. I wasn't lost in my thoughts or staring off into space as I had done for weeks at a time prior to the visitation from Jesus.

Three days later, I left my house, and I felt normal for the first time in weeks. I went to the church and spent several hours in my office. I remember kneeling to pray and, once again, all I could do was cry. On a couple of occasions, I simply sat on the floor in my office and cried for several hours. It was not a dreadful cry! I was overwhelmed with thankfulness that the torment and fear were gone. I simply could not successfully articulate the words *thank you*, so I cried. I believe God understood my admiration and appreciation for what He had done for me.

Over the next two weeks, it was as if I walked on a cloud. My mind was at rest, I was laughing, and some normalcy returned to our home. For the first time in weeks, I started thinking about our future and looking forward to things. I had experienced something remarkable, and it changed my life.

Several months following the visitation, I still thought about those few moments with Jesus every single day. I prayed and ask the Lord never to let me forget it, nor interpret it incorrectly. I also questioned within myself what the third banner represented. It had no writing on it, and Jesus didn't evaporate it by blowing on it as He did the other two banners. He wadded the third banner up as a paper ball and threw it at the demons.

Conquering the Chaos in Your Mind

Several years later, while I was in my office studying and praying for a Sunday message, an unusual presence of the Lord filled the room. Many times, while studying I will get excited about something I learn or some thought the Holy Spirit drops in my heart, but this moment was totally different. The tangible presence of the Lord came into the room. In fact, it was so tangible, I stopped studying and literally expected to see Jesus or an angel. I didn't, so I sat quietly. It was then I heard Jesus speak. I don't think I heard them with my physical ears, but they were so real and plain that it almost sounded audible.

He spoke these words:

"I am going to tell you now about the third banner. It represents the lie that Satan has used on people forever. You kept asking, 'Why is this happening to me?' Satan heard that question and answered it with this deception: 'You have done something sinful to bring this on yourself.' But you never were able to figure out anything you did even after confessing and asking forgiveness for everything you could remember multiple times."

Then the Lord reminded me of the dozens of people whom I have ministered to, prayed for, and talked with over the years who have all asked the same thing: "Have I committed an unpardonable sin and opened the door to this harassment?"

Do you also have this question? Are you tormented with the thought that you have done something sinful or wrong that has opened the door to harassment in your mind even though you've confessed and repented of everything you can think of that's wrong? *Stop!* It's a trick of the devil to keep you in doubt and fear.

Look at what Jesus said:

> *Nevertheless I tell you the truth. It is to your advantage that I go away; for if I do not go away, the Helper will not come to you; but if I depart, I will send Him to you. And when He has come, He will convict the world of sin, and of righteousness, and of judgment* (John 16:7-8).

Jesus said that when the Holy Spirit comes, He will convict or bring evidence of sin. Satan, however, accuses without evidence. If Satan can keep you questioning and doubting your righteousness in Christ, he will hinder you from exercising your rightful authority over him. If you think you must have done something you don't know about to cause the pain in your life, take that thought captive. It's a lie!

It's been a little over 30 years since my visitation from Jesus. But I can honestly say those two thoughts that harassed me the most and caused me such torment—*you are demon possessed* and *God does not love you*—are now so far removed from my thought life it's as if I never had them. They tried to get back into my mind, but their power was evaporated by the breath of Jesus!

Questions:

1. What are the lies the devil has tried to sell you that Jesus Himself would tell you are "vapors, smoke"?

Let me encourage you to jot down the lie and the scripture from God's Word that blows it away!

2. Satan accuses us without legitimate evidence. What is a good strategy to combat Satan's harassing accusations?

3. When was the last time you experienced a panic attack or thought battle in your mind? How did you move past that tormenting moment?

Prayer:

Heavenly Father, I thank You that according to Your Word in Luke 10:19, I have authority over all the power of the enemy. My mind belongs to me. It's not the property of fear, worry, and condemnation. Help me, Father, to stand against the attacks against my mind and refuse to believe Satan's illegitimate accusations against me. In Jesus' name, amen

Chapter 3

THE HELMET OF SALVATION: GOD'S PROTECTION FOR OUR MINDS

FOLLOWING THAT MONUMENTAL SATURDAY MORNING WHEN JESUS appeared to me, I experienced a few months of wonderful peace and rest in my mind. I was still trying to process the visitation and what it meant for several weeks afterward. I only told Amanda and a couple of ministry friends what had happened because it seemed too sacred to talk about. And to be honest, there was a sense of awe which continued to cover me like a blanket. I didn't want to say or do anything that would cause that blanket to fall off.

Within a month, I was back keeping regular office hours at church and busy with normal pastoral responsibilities—visiting the sick, networking with volunteers, and studying for three sermons a week. Oh yeah, back then, we went to church three times a week—Sunday morning, Sunday night, and Wednesday night. I was grateful that our lives were returning to normal.

I did notice during my devotions that the Bible was different to me. After the visitation from Jesus, the Bible was no longer just a book of great stories to preach about, but it had become a life force to me. It was as if God's Word was going through me instead of me going through God's Word. Every chapter I read was alive! I saw principles in the Word of God that I had never before seen. In fact, I started to enjoy reading the Bible so much I couldn't put it down.

A few more months passed, and everything was great. Our church was growing, and our toddler was full-sprint running. Life was good, and we were living the dream.

Then without warning, the horrible, tormenting thoughts started again. But it was different this time. Instead of paralyzing me when they came, their power and fear were less forceful. It seemed the condemning, accusatory thoughts had lost much of their sting.

> We cannot outthink Satan, but we can put him in retreat by our confession.

The actual thoughts were the same as before: *You are demon possessed. You are losing your mind. God doesn't love you. You are a phony.* But this time, these anxious thoughts trying to bully me were powerless. They couldn't penetrate or find a lodging place in my mind. They were on the outside trying to get in because

I was armed with truth this time. The truth Jesus shared with me—about thoughts being as vapors or smoke with no strength and power—served as my shield of faith to extinguish all the fiery darts of Satan.

When a negative thought tried to enter my mind, I would immediately remember what Jesus said to me and declare loudly, "That thought is a lie and has no power!" As soon as I would speak that out, the tormenting thought would retreat in obscurity.

> All Satan's schemes and strategies against us begin with a simple thought.

During that time, I learned a valuable truth about how to maintain control of our thought lives: We cannot outthink Satan, but we can put him in retreat by our confession.

The devil operates in the arena of thought. In fact, his modus operandi (MO) is thought control. Satan exerts his influence and power over people and nations by introducing thoughts into their minds.

Satan never deceives or convinces people to follow his way by approaching them personally in a red devil suit carrying a pitchfork. If he did, people would recognize him for who he is and resist him. Satan never telegraphs his temptations with a side note which says, "This moment is a life-destroying opportunity for you." If he cloaked his temptations with reality, we would never fall prey to them. No, Satan always introduces a temptation with a thought, and if we accept it, his deception begins. Think about this: all Satan's schemes and strategies against us begin with a simple thought.

We read a warning from the apostle Paul concerning the need to protect ourselves from the evil schemes and strategies of the devil. Paul told us one way we protect ourselves from Satan's devices is to suit up with the armor of God.

> ...Be strong in the Lord and in his mighty power. Put on all of God's armor so that you will be able to stand firm against all strategies of the devil. For we are not fighting against flesh-and-blood enemies, but against evil rulers and authorities of the unseen world, against mighty powers in this dark world, and against evil spirits in the heavenly places. Therefore, put on every piece of God's armor so you will be able to resist the enemy in the time of evil. Then after the battle you will still be standing firm. Stand your ground, putting on the belt of truth and the body armor of God's righteousness. For shoes, put on the peace that comes from the Good News so that you will be fully prepared. In addition to all of these, hold up the shield of faith to stop the fiery arrows of the devil. Put on salvation as your helmet, and take the sword of the Spirit, which is the word of God (Ephesians 6:10-17, NLT).

Paul named every piece of armor we are instructed to put on: the belt of truth (vs 14), the body armor of God's righteousness (or breastplate of righteousness as the NKJV refers to it) (vs 14), the shoes of peace (vs 15), the shield of faith (vs 16), the helmet of salvation (17), and the sword of the Spirit (vs 17). Without question, every piece of armor is valuable and necessary to stand against the wiles of the devil. But because of our topic, let's focus on the helmet of salvation. It protects our heads—our brains, our minds, our thought lives.

The helmet we are instructed to put on is not just any helmet but the helmet of salvation. The word *salvation* means "deliverance, safety, preservation, healing, and soundness." Literally, Paul instructed us to fill our minds with the knowledge of our deliverance, safety, preservation, healing, and soundness in Christ. When we do, we have protection against the devil when he tries to slip in accusatory, condemning, harassing, lustful, fearful, tempting, or tormenting thoughts into our minds.

After the visitation with Jesus, life was different for me because Jesus exposed the devil's lies. Jesus taught me the truths that I am teaching you. When Satan tried to gain access into my mind with his tormenting thoughts, he failed. My mind was covered with the truth of God's Word, which acted as a helmet of protection.

What Happens When We Don't Protect Our Minds

The Bible is full of people who made decisions that cost them dearly, simply because they did not protect their minds against the schemes of Satan. Let's consider some of these individuals and their behaviors so we can learn from their mistakes.

Ananias and Sapphira: Satan Filled Their Hearts

In Acts 5, the New Testament Church was young and growing. People were being prompted by the Holy Spirit to give away their houses, lands, and possessions in order for the less fortunate in the church to have sufficiency. One couple in the church, Ananias and Sapphira, heard about these acts of generosity and wanted to take part. So, they sold a possession and gave a portion of the money received to the apostles for distribution. Yet, they gave the impression to the church that they had given all the money to the apostles.

Apparently, the Holy Spirit revealed to Peter what the couple did. Peter called in Ananias and told him the possession belonged to him so he could sell it, not sell it, give away a portion, all, or none. The problem was not the amount given but the fact that Ananias and Sapphira lied. They gave the impression of doing one thing when they were actually doing another.

> The only way Satan influences our lives is pitching his deceptive thoughts.

Notice what Peter said to Ananias: "Ananias, why has Satan filled your heart to lie to the Holy Spirit and keep back part of the price of the land for yourself?" (Acts 5:3).

How did Satan fill the heart of Ananias? The devil didn't grab Ananias, pry open his chest, and pour deception into his heart. No, Satan filled Ananias with deception by introducing a deceptive thought. The devil operated in the arena of thought, and his tactics have not changed two thousand years later. The only way Satan influences our lives is pitching his deceptive thoughts. We, in turn, catch them and meditate upon them until they become our own.

Paul warned us of Satan's tactic and teaches us our defense in 2 Corinthians 10:

> *We capture rebellious thoughts and teach them*
> *to obey Christ* (Verse 5, NLT).

We must learn to examine every thought under the microscope of Christ and His Word. If a thought doesn't line up with the Word of God, we must take that thought captive and refuse to allow it to roam around in our minds.

This deception acted upon by Ananias and Sapphira ended up costing them their lives, and it all began with a single thought. Satan introduced a thought of deception into the couple's minds, and they accepted it. They didn't destroy it, reject it, or kick it out. They entertained it until it became their own thought and then acted upon it.

Simon the Sorcerer: 'The Thought of Your Heart'

Another familiar Bible story is found in Acts 8 involving Simon the sorcerer. A revival occurred in Samaria, and the whole region was turned upside down. People were saved, healed, and delivered from demon possession. Miracles, signs, and wonders took place continually through the ministry of Philip, the deacon.

Soon Peter and John traveled to Samaria to teach on receiving the Holy Spirit as they had received on the day of

Pentecost. As Peter and John laid hands on the Samaritans, the people began receiving the Holy Spirit. When Simon saw this supernatural phenomenon occurring, he offered Peter and John money to give him the gift of laying hands on people to receive the Holy Spirit.

We read in Acts 8:21 Peter's response, "You have neither part nor portion in this matter, for your heart is not right in the sight of God." The apostles discerned Simon's motives were impure and revealed that his heart was not right.

> One sinful thought embraced and acted upon has the power to destroy our lives.

Peter then gives us insight into what caused the contamination of Simon's heart:

Repent therefore of this your wickedness, and pray God if perhaps the thought of your heart may be forgiven you (Acts 8:22).

Simon had entertained and acted upon a sinful thought, and it motivated him to act in a way that brought God's displeasure. In fact, one sinful thought embraced and acted upon has the power to destroy our lives. We'll discuss this principle more in the chapters titled, "The Anatomy of a Stronghold—Part 1 and Part 2."

Counterattack Warning

My highest and best advice is never to leave home without your helmet of protection. In fact, neither should you remain home without it. Wearing your helmet of salvation at all times will save you from attacks and counterattacks and the torment they bring.

Over the years, dozens of well-meaning people have asked me, "Why did the thoughts return? If Jesus blew them, and they disappeared, why did they come back?"

Notice what the Bible tells us in Matthew 12:

> *When an unclean spirit goes out of a man, he goes through dry places, seeking rest, and finds none. Then he says, "I will return to my house from which I came." And when he comes, he finds it empty, swept, and put in order. Then he goes and takes with him seven other spirits more wicked than himself, and they enter and dwell there; and the last state of that man is worse than the first* (verses 43-45).

Unfortunately, Satan is more diligent than a lot of Christians. The gospel of Matthew gives us insight to Satan's persistence. Evil spirits, influences, and ideologies cannot produce their desired results without a habitation. To operate in the natural world, they must have natural partners. When an evil spirit has lost its effectiveness over a person or nation, it will seek out others. Before it eventually moves on for good, it will try again to return to its original habitation.

Jesus tells us that if our spirits or minds have not been filled with God's Word, the evil spirit or its influence will try again to gain entrance. The evil influence—deception or thought pattern—will return, and the last state of the person will then be worse than the first.

Over the years, I have laid hands on hundreds of people dealing with mental torment, runaway thoughts, and harassing memories. Because of the anointing, the thoughts and torment would retreat after hands were laid upon them. But I am always careful to tell them to fill their minds with God's Word and put on their helmets of salvation daily because the tormenting thoughts will try to return.

When the thoughts of torment surface again, speak and confess God's Word right then! Remember, we cannot outthink Satan, but we can put him in retreat by our confession.

We have been given a wonderful promise in 2 Timothy 1:7, "God has not given us a spirit of fear, but of power and of love and of a sound mind." If we get lazy or weary in the thought battle, eventually we will fall back under the influence of harassing thoughts. But if we are diligent to declare God's Word in answer to Satan's tormenting thoughts, we can keep harassing thoughts away.

Questions:

1. What is the devil's MO (modus operandi), and what is the arena where he does his dirty work?

2. How can you put the devil in retreat when he attacks your thought life?

3. How do all the devil's evil schemes begin?

Prayer:

Heavenly Father, I thank You according to Your Word in Isaiah 26:3 that You will keep me in perfect peace when my mind is fixed on You. Help me recognize when rogue and unhealthy thoughts try to slip into my pattern of thinking. Help me to immediately take those ungodly thoughts captive, so I can enjoy the peace of mind You have promised. In Jesus' name, amen.

Chapter 4

I WENT TO HEAVEN

A FEW MONTHS HAD PASSED AFTER MY VISITATION FROM JESUS, AND I had been diligent to keep my mind and heart filled with God's Word. Daily, I confessed scriptures over my life and endeavored to wear my helmet of salvation. I listened to worship music, and I chose not to let my thoughts wander off into nothingness. But one Wednesday afternoon, everything shifted.

All day the mental battle had been more intense as I prepared for my Wednesday night Bible study. I was physically tired, so my energy level wasn't the best. A couple of times during the day, I had entertained negative thoughts and experienced a few moments of heaviness. I was struggling to keep my mind focused on my lesson for the evening service. Realizing I was under attack, I ceased my study and simply knelt at my desk to pray.

Even though I was confessing God's Word in prayer, it seemed with each verse I confessed the harassing, evil thoughts became viler and louder. A strange dynamic was occurring. I was praying verbally from my heart and speaking God's Word, but my mind was pelted with terrible thoughts.

I remember this thought in particular swept across my mind: *Just give up and give in. You had a moment of peace, but you will never be completely free. You are not strong enough to remain free. Mental illness runs in your family, and this is your burden in life to bear. This is not demonic. It's genetic, and you can't change that.*

This might sound hard to believe, but for an instant, that series of thoughts gave me a sense of peace. *It's not my fault,* I thought. *I am not guilty. I am the victim.* For a moment, I was almost seduced into accepting it.

> The victim mentality is Satan tempting us to quit fighting for what God has promised us.

Let me stop right here and tell you that many people have fallen prey to this deception in their battle for the welfare of their minds. There is a deceptive peace and relief that comes when we believe we are victims. Being a victim gives us a legitimate excuse for the situation in which we find ourselves. As victims we are not responsible for the problem, and we are not responsible for the solution. The victim mentality is Satan tempting us to quit fighting for what God has promised us.

I often meet with people who have taken ownership of their emotional and mental harassment. They see a specialist who diagnoses them with a particular type of emotional or mental disorder. Once they receive the diagnostic label, they begin referring to it as "their problem, their bipolar, their schizophrenia." They take ownership, and it becomes their excuse.

When I have tried to encourage them by telling them that God wants to set them free and they don't have to live the rest of their lives depressed or mentally harassed, they get angry with me. The truth is, when they see themselves as victims, it removes their responsibility to fight for peace of mind.

A person's victim mentality becomes this: *God has promised me a sound mind. But if an emotional or mental disorder runs in my family, and my inflicted family members still love Jesus, then it's okay for me to have this issue and still be a Christian and go to heaven.*

No! That's not truth! It is a device of the devil. I experienced it myself. For a quick moment that Wednesday afternoon, the thoughts of enjoying God's peace of mind, a sound mind, a mind at rest, and a faith-filled mind gave way to the reasoning that mental torment runs in my family. I entertained the thought that since my family had survived, it was okay for me to struggle with thoughts. It was okay to live with them.

Suddenly, I realized those thoughts were not coming from inside where God's Spirit dwells but from the outside trying to get in. This wasn't God giving me relief or an answer to my dilemma. This wasn't the Lord speaking to me. This was Satan trying a different scheme.

Satan's tactic had changed.

He was no longer accusing me, and I was no longer on the defensive. He was now blaming others for my weakness: *Mental illness runs in your family. It's not demonic. It's genetic, and it's your burden in life to bear.*

A fraction of a moment passed, and I had realized where the thoughts were coming from and who their author was. I immediately rebuked the devil and his thoughts, and when I did the unbelievable occurred.

Without warning, I felt myself going upward, rising above my chair and then above my desk. I now know what the apostle Paul meant when he wrote about his vision in 2 Corinthians 12:2, saying, "I know a man in Christ who fourteen years ago—whether in the body I do not know, or whether out of the body I do not know, God knows—such a one was caught up to the third heaven."

I don't know if I went to heaven in my physical body or if it was an out of the body experience. But I do know that I felt myself ascending. It felt as though I was floating in air. I remember saying, "Oh, oh, oh!" as gravity lost its hold on me.

Then immediately I was standing in front of Jesus. It was totally different than when He visited me in the den of my home. The room we were in had no dimensions, and the brilliant colors all around I had never seen before. They were not simply colors on a color chart; they were colors that were alive with life itself—vivid and radiant.

I noticed there was movement in heaven, behind where Jesus was standing and around us. I don't know if they were angels or saints who were now heavenly residents. I have often thought back and wished I could have hit a pause button and looked around, but I was completely captivated by Jesus. His demeanor seemed different in heaven than when He appeared in my den. It was as if in my den, Jesus was on an assignment—He had come to get something done. In my den Jesus only spoke of what I was encountering, but in heaven He only voiced His love for me.

Though I had never experienced heaven before, I sensed an unbelievable feeling that I belonged there. It seemed like home. The feeling of acceptance and welcome was a huge contrast to all the lies Satan had been pelting my mind with—lies that Jesus didn't love me and that I had committed the unpardonable sin.

Jesus had the same appearance as when I saw Him before. His robe was the most brilliant white. His hair was the same length touching His shoulders. Jesus' eyes, oh His eyes, were the most beautiful I had ever seen. They glistened like a beautiful body of water that shimmers when a gentle breeze sweeps across its surface.

The very atmosphere of heaven was love. It was as if the air was liquid, and I was breathing liquid love. I felt an energy and life that I had never experienced before. My entire being was alive, and in that life was energy, peace, rests and contentment. If I could have remained in that place and moment forever, I would have been the happiest person ever born. Time and space were no more, and I had no concept of anything physical. The life and energy of heaven is love, and it surges through your being.

In dealing with the death of loved ones who have experienced a lengthy illness, family members will often say, "I wouldn't bring them back if I could. I know they are in a better place." I can tell you from personal experience that it is a far better place. The best moment on earth has nothing to compare to the continual life of heaven. I now understand why the apostle Paul said, "I'm torn between two desires: I long to go and be with Christ, which would be far better for me. But for your sakes, it is better that I continue to live" (Philippians 1:23-24, NLT). Paul had been caught up to heaven and had experienced the wonder and splendor of that enchanting place.

Heaven's beauty is breathtaking, and the residents don't live on oxygen. They live and move in an environment of perfect love

The challenge we have in explaining or telling others about heaven is that we have no comparisons on earth. Heaven's beauty is breathtaking, and the residents don't live on oxygen. They live and move in an environment of perfect love.

Jesus reached out and took my hands, saying, "I love you, son" and hugged me. When He embraced me, a feeling of purity, supernatural peace, fulfillment, and ecstatic joy surged through me. I remember moaning out loud from the feeling.

Jesus started to pull away, and instantly, I knew the moment was temporary and wasn't going to last long.

"I don't want to go," I said.

Jesus replied, "You must go back!"

I then said to Jesus, "I don't want to go back."

"Eddie, you must go back," Jesus answered. "You must go back for your wife and little boy and for them...."

Jesus glanced to His side, and as I followed his eyes, I saw a large room full of what appeared to be army cots. Though Jesus didn't verbalize it to me, I instantly knew the army cots represented fellow believers who had been wounded in the fight of faith. These cots would one day be filled with believers whose minds were being tormented due to the stresses and attacks of the enemy.

Jesus said once again, "Eddie, you must go back for them!"

I don't know how long I was in heaven, but I remember starting to pull away. I didn't walk away; it was as if a force pulled me back. Jesus never took His eyes off me. I never took my eyes off Him. Finally, I had been pulled back so far I couldn't see Jesus anymore. I realized I was back behind my desk, sitting on the floor in my office.

Needless to say, I didn't speak that night at church. In fact, Amanda had to help me walk to the car. She realized another encounter of some kind had occurred and simply drove me home. Three more days of crying took place. A blanket of peace and love covered me like a coat on my shoulders.

Two weeks later, a local pastor friend and I enjoyed a casual lunch together. Following lunch, he asked me to come by his office. I thought he wanted to show me a project he was working on at his church, but as I walked into his office, he asked me to sit down. For the next forty-five minutes, the pastor through tears shared with me the war he was fighting daily in his mind. As he said it, "All hell has come against my mind. I am having thoughts I've never had before, and I can't get them out of my mind." My heart broke as I heard him trying to frame the words to articulate his torment and brokenness. He told me things he hadn't been able to tell his wife and in no way could share with his church congregation—impure, condemning, and self-destructive thoughts.

As I listened to him pour out his heart, I immediately had a flashback of the scene in heaven of the army cots. I knew my reason for having to return to earth.

Now, many years later, Amanda and I have had the privilege of laying hands on hundreds and hundreds of individuals who struggle controlling their thought lives. In every conference and service where I teach what the Lord taught me during those visitations and what He continues to teach me now, people line up by the dozens for prayer. Each time I pray for people struggling with torment in their minds, I am reminded of the army cots and the soldiers on the battlefield who are wounded because of mental harassment.

Rogue thoughts and thought attacks are no respecter of persons. From the wealthy to the less fortunate, the famous to the unknown, the intelligent to the academic beginner, the young to the old, we all at times deal with anxiety, fear, and harassing thoughts that try to bully us and bring us down. Satan doesn't play fair. In fact, thought wars are not battles reserved for grown adults only. We are seeing more and more children seeking prayer as parents bring them to our services, seeking deliverance and peace from mental torment and harassment.

Experts tell us the average person processes between 50,000 and 60,000 thoughts a day.[3] There are 86,400 seconds in a day, so the average person is processing a thought every 1.3 seconds. We also are told that 90% of our thoughts tend to be repetitive. In other words, we think the same things over and over and over. It's easy to see how Satan can manipulate a person to unhealthy actions if a person thinks painful, anxious, tormenting, ungodly, and unhealthy thoughts 90% of the time.

Satan operates in the arena of thought, but God has promised us sound minds. God also has given us spiritual weapons to protect our minds against the tormenting schemes of the devil. In the next several chapters, I want to teach you how the Lord taught me to take control of my thought life and how you can also.

Questions:

❶. Why is the victim mentality both deceptive and dangerous?

❷. The very atmosphere of heaven is love. God wants us to know how much He loves us. What's a scripture about God's love for you that blesses you? Or take a moment to remember an encounter with the Lord in prayer where you have felt saturated by His love and peace.

Prayer:

Heavenly Father, I thank You according to Your Word in Romans 8:38-39 that absolutely nothing will be able to separate me from the love of God in Christ Jesus. Help me to settle forever in my mind that God loves me with an everlasting love. And to resist any thought or accusation that God is against me. I declare that I am the righteousness of God in Christ Jesus, and I have the mind of Christ. In Jesus' name, amen.

Chapter 5

THE ANATOMY OF A STRONGHOLD

Part 1

"HOW DID THIS HAPPEN?" THE BEAUTIFUL THIRTY-SEVEN-YEAR-OLD wife and mother of two asked me as she wiped the tears from her face. She and her husband made an appointment to come see me. They were members of our church family and actively involved in various ministry opportunities. They were a beautiful family with two darling and brilliant children. He had a wonderful job in the manufacturing industry, and she was an educator. They seemed to be doing well financially. Their children were involved in extracurricular activities and sports, so from the outside, life appeared to be good.

But this visit wasn't a time of celebration. He sat quietly, as his wife began by asking the question, "How did this happen, Pastor?"

"How did what happen?" I replied.

She immediately buried her head in her hands and through the tears said, "I have been unfaithful to my husband."

She began recounting every good thing she had done and been involved in. She said, "I love Jesus and have been serving Him since I was a child. I am married to my college sweetheart and have been blessed with two of the most wonderful children ever born. I have never done this type of thing before, so why did I do this?"

We talked about repentance and forgiveness. Her husband opened up and shared his feelings of betrayal, hurt, and embarrassment. We prayed together and talked extensively. Knowing this type of wound is not easily healed, we made an appointment to meet again the following week to see how they were doing.

Before they left, she asked again, "Pastor, how did this happen? I love Jesus and my family."

Immediately, I started replaying the scenario. "You guys have been busy working, traveling, and playing. It was not intentional. But if I were a betting man, I would say that space developed between you and your husband and even between you and your relationship with the Lord. Then one day, probably after a disagreement, a coworker complimented you in the break room, and it felt good to receive a compliment. A few days later, he complimented you again.

This time, you entertained the compliment and thought about it several minutes, remembering it had been a while since your husband had commented on your appearance. It felt good to be complimented and made to feel attractive and desirable.

"Over the next few days, you replayed his compliments in your mind and started hoping you would see him again in the break room. Eventually, the passing greetings in the break room turned into casual conversations, and the casual conversations turned into personal conversations."

Then, I shared how the idea of meeting outside of work for coffee or a drink finally was made. On the surface it seemed innocent, but the scheme for betrayal was well underway.

The Holy Spirit would bring a thought of conviction, and when He did, she promised the Lord in prayer she would stop and never see him outside of work again. But on and on, the persistent thoughts and imaginations of being with him bombarded her mind. Finally, the images of being with him became a stronghold that consumed her thought life.

She stopped me and asked, "Pastor, who told you what happened?"

"No one told me anything," I said. "In fact, I had no idea you were involved in this situation until you walked into this office and revealed it. But I know how Satan works, and he has no new tactics." As I continued, she and her husband sat in disbelief as I replayed the deceptive scenario almost to perfection.

This wife did not wake up one morning and decide to injure her marriage and hurt her witness for Christ by committing adultery. In fact, if you suggested she do that, she would have told you that you were crazy. She did not flippantly decide to betray her marriage vows and bring shame and reproach against her good name.

Likewise, people bound by substance abuse do not on a whim decide to become addicted to drugs or alcohol. The same goes for folks with a stronghold of fear, lust, or anything else Satan uses to create a stronghold in us. It doesn't happen automatically. It can't happen instantly. A stronghold in a person's life takes time to develop, and it begins with a thought.

> A stronghold in a person's life takes time to develop, and it begins with a thought.

Understanding the Nature of a Stronghold

Let's look at this scripture below where the apostle Paul gives us his insight into mental strongholds.

For though we walk in the flesh, we do not war according to the flesh. For the weapons of our warfare are not carnal but mighty in God for pulling down strongholds, casting down arguments and every high thing that exalts itself against the knowledge of God, bringing every thought into captivity to the obedience of Christ (2 Corinthians 10:3-5).

First of all, we must understand what a stronghold is. The word *stronghold* in the verse above is the Greek word *ochuroma*, which means "a fortress or that which is firm."

One of my favorite authors, Rick Renner, wrote in his book *Sparkling Gems from the Greek Volume 1* the following:

> By the time of the New Testament, the word *ochuroma* also came to be the very same Greek word used to describe a prison. Since the most secure, highly guarded prisons were usually constructed deep inside such fortresses, it makes sense that the word for a fortress or stronghold is the same identical Greek word used to picture a prison. Whereas a fortress keeps outsiders from getting in, a prison keeps insiders from getting out. Prisons are places of detention or holding tanks.... They are designed to hold a prisoner in captivity.[4]

Rick goes on to say this:

> The strongholds Paul refers to are lies that the devil has ingrained so deeply in your mind and your belief system that they now exert power over certain areas of your life.... As a result, the person under mental or emotional assault is held captive like a prisoner to those lies. He sits behind mental and emotional bars, viewing life through the illusion of bondage that Satan has put into his mind.[4]

Whereas much of the teaching on strongholds over the years has emphasized "strongholds in the heavenlies," the apostle Paul informed us that the place or the prison that poses the greatest danger to a person's life is in his or her mind and emotions. A stronghold is a compulsion, a habit, a continual pattern of thinking that keeps a person in bondage or prohibits him or her from being everything God desires for the person to be. It's a fortress, a citadel, a prison of mental anguish.

My dear friend the late Terry Law explains that a stronghold can be anything Satan uses in our lives to hinder us from experiencing God's best. It can be one of the dozens of fears or phobias known to mankind. It can be an insecurity that frightens us, a past tragedy that haunts us, or an uncontrollable lust that drives us. It can be substance abuse, sexual addiction, or greed. It can be emotional trauma caused by a childhood incident or a host of other things.

Satan's goal is to develop a formidable stronghold in your life. If he can create a stronghold in your mind or emotions, he can imprison you. But just as modern-day fortresses and prisons must be built over time, Satan's strongholds in your life are built over time as well. Satan does not have the power or authority to develop a stronghold at his will. He cannot just fling a stronghold on you anytime he chooses. He doesn't have that type of authority or power.

So how does he do it?

The devil is not a creative being—he's just a thief and a robber. So, every good idea and effective tactic in his arsenal, he stole from God. In other words, Satan has simply stolen the system of God's kingdom and uses it to create his kingdom of darkness in people's lives. Therefore, the more we understand about how God's kingdom works, the wiser we'll be to the devil's deceptive devices against us.

The Kingdom-of-God Process

In the gospel of Mark, Jesus detailed how the kingdom of God is established in our lives. The first thing He explained is that the whole kingdom is established or developed by a process. Unfortunately, *process* is not a word we like in the church world. The Bible stories we remember and favor the most are the ones that describe the sudden happenings of God. For example, the modern church age began after a suddenly of God.

> *When the Day of Pentecost had fully come, they were all with one accord in one place. And suddenly there came a sound from heaven, as of a rushing mighty wind, and it filled the whole house where they were sitting* (Acts 2:1-2).

The Holy Spirit suddenly filled the believers waiting on God's promise. We love it when God does a sudden work, but to the surprise of many Christians, that is *not* how the kingdom of God develops in our daily lives. It doesn't happen suddenly; it develops through consistent effort.

Here's another famous suddenly of God:

Then Saul, still breathing threats and murder against the disciples of the Lord, went to the high priest and asked letters from him to the synagogues of Damascus, so that if he found any who were of the Way, whether men or women, he might bring them bound to Jerusalem. As he journeyed, he came near Damascus, and suddenly a light shone around him from heaven. Then he fell to the ground, and heard a voice saying to him, "Saul, Saul, why are you persecuting Me?" (Acts 9:1-4).

Nothing is more thrilling than seeing the Holy Spirit do a sudden work in a person's life. A sudden healing, a sudden revelation, a sudden deliverance is the most exciting thing to witness in all the world, but again, the kingdom of God is not established in our lives that way.

While the born-again experience is a sudden work, developing the kingdom of God in our lives requires our time and involvement. It's not immediate but progressive.

> Developing the kingdom of God in our lives requires our time and involvement. It's not immediate but progressive.

In fact, I have watched numerous God-fearing friends get out of faith because an answer to a prayer, a healing, or a deliverance did not take place immediately. When the answer did not arrive quickly, these dear people would get in doubt, unbelief, or disappointment and question God.

The writer of Hebrews reminds us of a vitally important step in receiving from God:

> *Therefore do not cast away your confidence, which has great reward. For you have need of endurance, so that after you have done the will of God, you may receive the promise* (Hebrews 10:35-36).

We are reminded that after we have done the will of God, after we have prayed effectively, and after we have been obedient, we must walk in endurance and patience. The answer will come, but it may not arrive suddenly. If the answer does come suddenly, that's wonderful, but that's the exception, not the rule.

Another verse along this same line is found in Hebrews:

> The combination of faith and patience creates the environment for the promises of God to be realized and the kingdom of God to develop in our lives.

> *...do not become sluggish, but imitate those who through faith and patience inherit the promises* (Hebrews 6:12).

We enjoy talking about faith, hearing about faith, and reading about faith, but faith has a partner we seldom hear about or desire to hear about called patience. The combination of faith and patience creates the environment for the promises of God to be realized and the kingdom of God to develop in our lives.

'First the Blade, Then the Ear...'

Notice the principles Jesus revealed about how the kingdom of God develops in our lives. I really like how the
passage is written in the King James Version:

> *And he said, So is the kingdom of God, as if
> a man should cast seed into the ground; and
> should sleep, and rise night and day, and the
> seed should spring and grow up, he knoweth
> not how. For the earth bringeth forth fruit of
> herself; first the blade, then the ear, after that
> the full corn in the ear. But when the fruit
> is brought forth, immediately he putteth in
> the sickle, because the harvest is come* (Mark
> 4:26-29, KJV).

The kingdom of God is not developed in our lives by
a suddenly of God. Jesus did not say we plant the Word in
our hearts, and suddenly, we enjoy all the benefits of the
kingdom. No, Jesus stated plainly that we plant the Word
in our hearts and then the process begins. *Over time* the
seed begins to grow, and fruit *eventually* appears as it's
nourished. There's no suddenly about it.

As I shared earlier, in the early days of our little church
in Algood, the resources were lean. We learned to pray
that familiar passage in the famous Lord's Prayer that says,
"Give us this day our daily bread," because we didn't live
from week to week; we lived from day to day.

So instead of starving, we decided to try our hand at
gardening. I asked a neighbor to bring his tiller over to my

house and turn up a small garden spot about 30 x 30 feet. Then Amanda and I went to the local co-op and asked the manager for suggestions on what to plant. He suggested green beans, tomatoes, a bunch of potatoes, squash, and okra. So that's what we bought.

We spent an entire Friday working in our little garden. We planted every seed we had and each tomato slip. We watered each plant and added some nutrients to each seed spot. On our hands and knees, we crawled through the garden making sure there were no weeds or hard-packed dirt that would prohibit our seeds from coming up. After we finished, we held hands and asked the Lord to bless our garden. We reached our hands out over our garden spot and declared it was blessed and our seed would produce fruit. Dirty and tired, Amanda and I walked hand in hand into our little home, feeling a great sense of satisfaction and expectancy.

The next morning, I awoke to the sun shining through the window. As I got out of bed and walked by the bedroom window, something caught my attention. I did a double take! Something was in our garden! I walked to the window and looked outside, but I couldn't believe what I saw. In our little garden we had just planted, I saw what appeared to be a full-grown watermelon, a couple of cantaloupes, several cucumbers spread out, and what appeared to be a head of cabbage. I rubbed my eyes and looked again. Sure enough, those fruits and vegetables were lying in my garden.

Excitedly, I yelled for Amanda to get up and come look. She jumped out of bed thinking something was wrong and walked to the window. "Look what's in our garden!" I said.

As she was looking and laughing, I had already run for the back door to go outside and get a firsthand look. As I trotted down to the garden spot, my mind was racing with all types of thoughts. *God has done a miracle! Our prayer of faith has worked! This is going to be a remarkable story!* But the closer I got to our garden I noticed what appeared to be the footprints of sneakers and shoes in the dirt all around the garden spot.

By that time, Amanda walked up beside me laughing. Then it dawned on me, some of our friends who heard what we were doing came over during the night and put those things in our garden. The joke was on us!

After laughing for a few minutes, I realized how silly I must have looked running outside in such excitement. Anyone who has a half a brain knows you don't plant okra and get a harvest of cucumbers. You don't plant tomatoes and get potatoes. And you definitely don't plant squash and get cabbage. In addition to that, every gardener knows you don't plant on Friday and get a harvest on Saturday. It takes time for the seed to produce the desired results.

Likewise, the benefits of the kingdom of God are developed in our lives by the kingdom *process*—first the blade, then the ear, then the full corn in the ear. The fruit, the harvest, and the results don't happen overnight.

Over the years, I have been guilty of unearthing my faith seed because I became weary during the process. I would plant God's promise in my heart, but after a few days of waiting and seeing no results, I would stop watering my seed or simply forget about it and let the weeds overtake it. But I'm so thankful for God's Word that tells us exactly how to plant good seed in good soil and keep it growing into an abundant harvest.

Power Seed and the Soil It Needs

The kingdom process is such a valuable truth that Jesus referred to it throughout the entire chapter of Mark 4 where He taught on the process, the soil, and the seed.

> *Listen! Behold, a sower went out to sow. And it happened, as he sowed, that some seed fell by the wayside; and the birds of the air came and devoured it.*
>
> *And these are the ones by the wayside where the word is sown. When they hear, Satan comes immediately and takes away the word that was sown in their hearts* (Mark 4:3-4, 15).

The seed is the Word of God, and Satan stole the seed in the person represented in these verses before the kingdom process even had a chance to get started. Obviously, if the seed never gets planted, there will never be a harvest.

For example, have you ever attended a church service on a Sunday morning and enjoyed the worship and were stirred by the pastor's sermon, but later that day when someone asked you what the minister preached about, you couldn't remember? Satan hates the seed of God's Word, so the last thing the devil wants is for you to allow God's Word—the seed—to be planted in your heart and begin growing. Have you noticed that you wake up feeling more tired on Sunday mornings than any other day of the week? And if you are looking for a family feud, you can easily find one on Sunday morning before church. Why? Satan doesn't want you receiving the seed of God's Word.

In fact, whole nations, governments, or regimes under demonic influence prohibit the Bible from being distributed or Christians from gathering to worship. They spend millions of dollars penalizing and persecuting people who own Bibles or believe in the Bible. Why would a nation with millions of people and billions of dollars be frightened by one book? What is it about this one little book that causes governments to use their military might to seek out and destroy anyone who possess a Bible?

Your Bible is a weapon more powerful than any weapon a nation possesses. It's precious and eternal seed in your hands. 1 Peter 1:23 says, "Having been born again, not of corruptible seed but incorruptible, through the word of God which lives and abides forever." This incorruptible seed is unlike any other seed, because when it is planted, it will produce a harvest that changes generations for an eternity.

Satan hates your Bible! He cannot stand this precious seed because he has absolutely no might against it. He works overtime against this weapon of God—keeping you from getting the seed planted in your heart and hindering you from learning how to use your weapon.

Stony Ground

> *Some fell on stony ground, where it did not have much earth; and immediately it sprang up because it had no depth of earth. But when the sun was up it was scorched, and because it had no root it withered away* (Mark 4:5-6).
>
> *These likewise are the ones sown on stony ground who, when they hear the word, immediately receive it with gladness; and they have no root in themselves, and so endure only for a time. Afterward, when tribulation or persecution arises for the word's sake, immediately they stumble* (Mark 4:16-17).

In this person, the seed gets planted, but Satan brings trouble to disturb the kingdom process from being completed, and the person never enjoys the benefits of God's kingdom. So often, we find a truth from God's Word—a principle of faith or a promise in scripture—that is the answer to our present situation, and we begin standing on that promise. But as soon as we do, it seems every difficulty imaginable is turned loose against us. Numerous times I have been approached by good Christians relaying this very thing.

So don't be surprised when problems, disappointments, and delays surface after you hear a truth that helps you and you act on it. Satan is trying to steal the seed or distract you from guarding God's seed that you have placed in your heart. Why? The devil understands he must stop the kingdom process or the seed will bring forth fruit in your life.

Thorny Ground

> *And some seed fell among thorns; and the thorns grew up and choked it, and it yielded no crop* (Mark 4:7).
>
> *Now these are the ones sown among thorns; they are the ones who hear the word, and the cares of this world, the deceitfulness of riches, and the desires for other things entering in choke the word, and it becomes unfruitful* (Mark 4:18-19).

This person allows thorns to grow with the precious seed, and during the process, the thorns corrupt the precious seed. Jesus identified the thorns as the cares of the world, the deceitfulness of riches, and the desire for things. These people are the ones who have allowed other things of life to compete for control of their hearts.

Now remember, these are wonderful people who love God. They are sowing God's Word in their hearts, but the Word doesn't take priority over other things competing for their time and attention. Other things eventually consume the ground and overrun the precious seed of God's Word. These same folks will often say, "I tried that faith stuff, but it didn't work for me." Yet, in reality, we often don't receive from God or enjoy the fulfillment of His promises because other things in our lives have taken first place.

Give the Word Full Attention

Another way of understanding this truth is realizing that the seed of God itself is under attack. If Satan cannot keep the seed from being planted in our hearts, he will unleash an onslaught of trouble, difficulties, or distractions against us to get our focus on those things—*anything* but the promises of God's Word.

Paul warned young Timothy of this temptation:

> *Until I come, devote yourself to the public reading of Scripture, to preaching and to teaching. Do not neglect your gift, which was given you through prophecy when the body of elders laid their hands on you. Be diligent in these matters; give yourself wholly to them, so that everyone may see your progress. Watch your life and doctrine closely. Persevere in them, because if you do, you will save both yourself and your hearers* (1 Timothy 4:13-16, NIV).

Paul instructed Timothy to devote himself to maintaining the teaching and modeling what he had experienced and witnessed. He told him to be diligent and give God's Word his full attention.

King Solomon, a man gifted with supernatural wisdom, gave the same admonition in the Old Testament:

> *My son, give attention to my words; Incline your ear to my sayings. Do not let them depart from your eyes; Keep them in the midst of your heart;*

> *For they are life to those who find them, And*
> *health to all their flesh* (Proverbs 4:20-22).

Even though written hundreds of years apart, these messages are the same: the Word of God should be first place in your life.

I love how the Living Bible translates this verse:

> *Listen, son of mine, to what I say. Listen care-*
> *fully. Keep these thoughts ever in mind; let*
> *them penetrate deep within your heart, for*
> *they will mean real life for you and radiant*
> *health* (Proverbs 4:20-22, TLB).

Once again, we find an admonition to keep our thoughts filled with the Word of God. Again, this is not a New Testament verse but written several thousand years ago. God has always emphasized the need to keep our minds focused properly. This verse also gives us amazing insight to the path both truth and deception must travel to form our beliefs.

Focus on the phrase, "Keep these thoughts ever in mind." It does not mean you should carry around an open Bible everywhere you go. The point is remembering God's Word, committing God's Word to memory, and keeping God Word's in the forefront of your mind.

A Good Harvest

> *But other seed fell on good ground and yielded*
> *a crop that sprang up, increased and produced:*

some thirtyfold, some sixty, and some a hundred.

But these are the ones sown on good ground, those who hear the word, accept it, and bear fruit: some thirtyfold, some sixty, and some a hundred (Mark 4:8, 20).

This person plants God's Word in his or her life, and over time, the seed grows and produces a harvest. But it's important to remember that this person persisted through the difficulties and distractions that the other three hearers didn't navigate successfully. This person guarded the seed, understood difficulty was an attempt to steal the seed, and gave the seed first priority in his or her life.

> The benefits of the kingdom of God are available to everyone but receiving the benefits is determined by how well we defend and navigate the process of seed growth.

Ultimately, God's Word produced a crop of fruit and benefits in this person's life.

This person won the battle in his or her thought life and kept God's Word as the primary focus. Satan tried every trick in his arsenal to steal the seed, but this person didn't fall for his tricks or allow the thief to win. Jesus taught that the benefits of the kingdom of God are available to everyone but receiving the benefits is determined by how well we defend and navigate the process of seed growth.

Questions:

1. What is a stronghold? Give a few examples of strongholds that have tried to attack you or a loved one.

2. Can the devil fling a stronghold at you at his will? Why or why not?

3. How do strongholds develop?

Prayer:

Heavenly Father, I thank You according to Your Word in 2 Corinthians 10:4 that You have given us spiritual weapons that are strong enough to pull down the strongholds of Satan. Help me to daily keep my helmet of salvation on, remembering my righteousness and authority in Christ. Help me to take every rogue thought captive and win the battle for my mind. In Jesus' name, amen.

Chapter 6

THE ANATOMY OF A STRONGHOLD

Part 2

WHILE SATAN CANNOT COME UP WITH ANYTHING ORIGINAL, HE IS A master of perversion. Anything effective he does was stolen from God and turned from good to evil. Therefore, just as the kingdom of God operates by process, the kingdom of darkness operates by process as well. Satan simply stole the seed-growth process and uses it to establish his strongholds in our lives.

That's what happened to me. During the season of oppressions and bondage I experienced, I repeatedly asked the Lord how I came to the place of being bound by fear. How did I get to the point that I would not leave my house for days at a time because of fear and paranoia?

81

I remember telling the Lord that I had always been a good boy. I grew up in church, and my granddad was the pastor of our church. I did not do the sinful things that some of my classmates did in high school. I knew from a child that I wanted to be in ministry. It didn't seem fair that this harassment and torment had invaded my life. Where had I opened the door? What had I done to reap this type of harassment?

It was during those darkest moments when my mind would not shut off and tormenting thoughts paralyzed me that the Lord began to show me from His Word how strongholds get established in our lives.

The apostle Paul informed us that though we walk in the flesh, our battle is not a fleshly one. As Christians, we are involved in spiritual warfare, and therefore, we should understand we are opposed by a spiritual enemy.

> *For though we walk in the flesh, we do not war according to the flesh. For the weapons of our warfare are not carnal but mighty in God for pulling down strongholds, casting down arguments and every high thing that exalts itself against the knowledge of God, bringing every thought into captivity to the obedience of Christ* (2 Corinthians 10:3-5).

Notice also how Paul identified our spiritual enemy when he wrote to the church at Ephesus.

> *Finally, my brethren, be strong in the Lord and in the power of His might. Put on the whole*

armor of God, that you may be able to stand against the wiles of the devil. For we do not wrestle against flesh and blood, but against principalities, against powers, against the rulers of the darkness of this age, against spiritual hosts of wickedness in the heavenly places (Ephesians 6:10-12).

Paul made it clear in both passages that we are in a struggle with unseen evil forces. The goal of these unseen evil forces is to hinder and prohibit God's plans and purposes from coming to pass in our lives. One of the ways they accomplish their goal is by developing strongholds in our minds and emotions. But these evil forces don't have the power to randomly inflict us with a stronghold anytime they choose. They are powerless against us when we are suited up with our spiritual armor and have a working knowledge of God's Word.

> Evil forces don't have the power to randomly inflict us with a stronghold anytime they choose.

Lurking Outside the Door

An interesting truth is found in the Old Testament book of Genesis that reveals how Satan is always lurking around and waiting for an opening into our lives.

Now Adam knew Eve his wife, and she conceived and bore Cain, and said, "I have acquired a man from the Lord." Then she bore again, this time his brother Abel. Now Abel was a keeper of sheep, but Cain was a tiller of the ground. And in the process of time it came to pass that Cain brought an offering of the fruit of the ground to the Lord. Abel also brought of the firstborn of his flock and of their fat. And the Lord respected Abel and his offering, but He did not respect Cain and his offering. And Cain was very angry, and his countenance fell. So the Lord said to Cain, "Why are you angry? And why has your countenance fallen? If you do well, will you not be accepted? And if you do not do well, sin lies at the door. And its desire or you, but you should rule over it" (Genesis 4:1-7).

Cain and Abel, the first two sons of Adam and Eve, brought their offerings to the Lord. The Lord accepted Abel's offering but did not accept Cain's offering. Verse 6 above says that Cain became "very angry and his countenance fell," or in other words, he looked depressed and dejected.

Notice how the Lord responded to Cain and said, "If you do well, you will be accepted, but if you do not do well, *sin lies at the door"* (verse 7).

It's interesting to note that sin doesn't have the authority or ability to knock down your door and barge in. Sin and sinful influence remain lurking around and waiting outside your door. You are the one who opens the door to sinful influence, either through negligence, temptation, or ignorance.

How did Cain open the door? We know that Cain's anger and jealousy eventually took over, and he killed his brother, Abel. But people just don't wake up one morning after being disappointed and kill their family members. Something had to transpire in Cain's mind and heart to push him to the point of killing his only brother.

Jesus told us how the door to sin is opened:

> *...Do you not yet understand that whatever enters the mouth goes into the stomach and is eliminated? But those things which proceed out of the mouth come from the heart, and they defile a man. For out of the heart proceed evil thoughts, murders, adulteries, fornications, thefts, false witness, blasphemies. These are the things which defile a man, but to eat with unwashed hands does not defile a man* (Matthew 15:17-20).

Jesus taught that eating food and dining without washing our hands will not defile us spiritually. Of course, eating unhealthy food is not good for us naturally, and eating without washing our hands is not sanitary. But neither of these things affect our spiritual health. Jesus goes on to say that words that come out of our mouths are the fruit of what's in our hearts.

In verse 19, Jesus revealed one of the most insightful truths in scripture. He said the things that defile a man are the things that come from the heart, and He listed some of them: "For out of the heart proceed evil thoughts, murders, adulteries, fornications, thefts, false witness, blasphemies."

Did you notice the first thing Jesus mentioned that comes from a defiled man are *evil thoughts*? He named several sins we are familiar with, but evil thoughts top the list. In fact, murder begins with a thought. Thefts begin with a thought. Adultery begins with a thought. That's the reason I was able to recount to the young couple what caused the betrayal of their marriage vows because it all begins with a thought.

Think of it this way. We never have to be fearful of being unfaithful to our spouse if we never entertain thoughts of unfaithfulness. Murder, fornication, theft, lying, or anything else Satan tempts us with will never gain a foothold in our lives if we don't allow it room to roam unchecked in our minds.

> All intentional sins begin with a single thought. If we stop the thought, we prohibit the action.

I grew up hearing a phrase similar to this: "It doesn't matter what you think, if you don't act on it." But it does matter! It matters because our thoughts lead to actions. In fact, all intentional sins begin with a single thought. If we stop the thought, we prohibit the action.

My original question was, "How did Cain open the door to sin and eventually murder?" The answer is that Cain became angry at what God said, and Satan suggested the thought of murder. Cain accepted that thought, entertained that thought, and the door opened. Right then, the kingdom-of-darkness process began.

Jesus said before a person commits murder, murderous thoughts first must be embraced and entertained. Remember, Satan operates in the arena of thought. He lies outside the door of your life, always looking for an opportunity to suggest a thought which will move you away from the plan and purpose of God. If you allow space for evil, fearful, revengeful, or lustful thoughts to roam in your mind, you have opened the door to sin.

This is the reason Paul told the Corinthians "... bringing every thought into captivity to the obedience of Christ" (2 Corinthians 10:5). We keep the door to sin shut in our lives by taking our thoughts captive.

So why did I experience hellish torment in my mind and live a prisoner of fear in my house for a year? My lack of knowledge of God's Word allowed a rogue thought to get in my mind, and the process of darkness began.

For years I had allowed lustful, fearful, and negative thoughts in my mind. Even as a pastor, I had been taught what to wear, where to go and where not to go, the correct length of my hair, and all the things we errantly thought made a person holy, but I never remember anyone teaching me what to think.

Is that important? Unquestionably, yes! God tell us, "For as he thinks in his heart, so is he" (Proverbs 23:7).

All my problems started with the single thought, *You must be demon possessed.* If I had stopped that one thought in its tracks, I would have derailed and escaped years of heartache and torment.

The Kingdom-of-Darkness Process

It's a wonderful thing to be delivered from bondage and strongholds—prisons of torment and addiction—but it's an even greater thing never to be imprisoned by a stronghold at all. That's why God shows us how the devil works so we can resist him and overcome him. Paul said, "So that Satan will not outsmart us...we are familiar with his evil schemes" (2 Corinthians 2:11, NLT).

In the previous chapter, we discussed the kingdom-of-God process detailed in Mark 4, which is first the blade, then the ear, and finally the full corn in the ear. Now let's look at how Satan perverts the process, which 2 Corinthians 10 tells us is first the thought, then the imagination, and finally the stronghold.

It has been there all along, but we have failed to see it. We have rebuked the devil, bound the devil, cast out the devil, and cast off the devil. We have treated the devil as some almighty force that requires all our energy to overcome every day of our lives. Many preachers and teachers spend more time talking about the devil than they do talking about God or His Word. Listen, folks! Satan is a defeated foe, and his only viable weapon against us is deception.

Jesus gave us the winning response to Satan's weapon, "If you abide in My word, you are My disciples indeed. And you shall know the truth, and the truth shall make you free" (John 8:31-32).

The Spirit-filled Church has prided itself on the power to pull down strongholds, which is wonderful. But at the same time, we have unconsciously given the impression that our enemy has equal power. He certainly does not! His efforts to set up addictions, chaos, and shameful sin in our lives can be defeated easily when we learn the simple truth about maintaining a godly thought life.

> Satan is a defeated foe, and his only viable weapon against us is deception.

Let's look again at this all-important scripture about mind battles that the Holy Spirit spoke through the apostle Paul.

For though we walk in the flesh, we do not war according to the flesh. For the weapons of our warfare are not carnal but mighty in God for pulling down strongholds, casting down arguments and every high thing that exalts itself against the knowledge of God, bringing every thought into captivity to the obedience of Christ (2 Corinthians 10:3-5).

Notice in verse 4 that our weapons are for the pulling down of strongholds. In other words, the stronghold already has been set up and established, so the spiritual weapon is needed to pull it down and demolish it. We've also learned that the stronghold didn't get set up overnight or without our permission or involvement. It takes a process for a stronghold to be established in our lives, and verses 3-4 tell us it is first the thought, then the imagination, and finally the stronghold.

The Thought Comes First

As previously shared, I've heard unassuming people say it doesn't matter what you think as long as you don't act upon it. But we've learned that the thoughts we entertain eventually become the actions and behaviors we demonstrate. Plain and simple, our thoughts determine our actions. That's why it's so important to discipline and guard our thought lives.

Years ago, I heard this statement, which has remained with me: "Thoughts are blueprints for actions." The things you continually think about today will become your words, actions, and attitudes tomorrow. What you think about is important, and the Bible has something to say about it.

> *Finally, brethren, whatsoever things are true, whatsoever things are honest, whatsoever things are just, whatsoever things are pure, whatsoever things are lovely, whatsoever things are of good report; if there be any virtue, and if there be any praise, think on these things* (Philippians 4:8, KJV).

In this verse, Paul specifically told you what to think and what type of thoughts you should allow in your mind. Why? Because your thought life is the first door Satan penetrates to develop a stronghold in your life.

The prophet Isaiah understood the importance of a guarded thought life when he wrote this:

> *You will keep in perfect peace all who trust in you, all whose thoughts are fixed on you!* (Isaiah 26:3, NLT).

God revealed to the world through the prophet Isaiah how wrong thoughts serve as enemies to the plans and purposes of God for our lives.

> *Let the wicked forsake his way, and the unrighteous man his thoughts; let him return to the Lord, and He will have mercy on him; and to our God, for He will abundantly pardon* (Isaiah 55:7).

God demands the wicked forsake their way but also their thoughts, because thoughts eventually lead to actions. I learned that I could repent of my sinful actions, but if I continued entertaining sinful thoughts, eventually I would need to repent of those same sinful actions again.

> Your thought life is the first door Satan penetrates to develop a stronghold in your life.

The books we read, the programs we watch, and the music we listen to all carry thoughts of life and death. Therefore, we must continually guard our thought lives. In reality, guarding our thought gateway is a daily discipline, not a once-a-week event.

Satan knows that he must penetrate your thoughts before he can exercise any influence in your life. So, he will continually bring rogue thoughts, lustful thoughts, negative thoughts, condemning thoughts, doubtful thoughts, and fearful thoughts to your mind. The devil continually pitches his thoughts to see if one will penetrate and find a lodging place in your mind.

This is why you must take every negative thought captive!

At first this spiritual discipline can be a real struggle, especially if you have had no boundaries on your thought life. Before I learned the value of having a disciplined thought life, I allowed my mind to roam and fantasize on a lot of ungodly images and thoughts. So, getting my mind under control was a challenge, but eventually I was able to get my thought life back under the Lordship of Christ. And you can, too!

The Imagination Comes Second

If we don't bring discipline to our minds and control our thought lives, ungodly thoughts will turn into imaginations or what we commonly refer to as fantasies. Imagination is powerful—it can create positive, godly images or negative, perverse ones.

For example, God told Abram (later called Abraham) to dream and imagine the size of his family, and God brought that image to pass.

And the Lord said to Abram, after Lot had separated from him: "Lift your eyes now and look from the place where you are—northward, southward, eastward, and westward; for all the land which you see I give to you and your descendants forever. And I will make your descendants as the dust of the earth; so that if a man could number the dust of the earth, then your descendants also could be numbered. Arise, walk in the land through its length and its width, for I give it to you" (Genesis 13:14-17).

Dreaming God dreams and imagining God ideas are one way we keep ourselves stirred up and moving toward God's plan for our lives, but at the same time, ungodly images and fantasies keep our flesh stirred up and moving toward strongholds in our lives. Strongholds begin with a thought, and ungodly thoughts not arrested and taken captive will grow and turn into imaginations.

The Old Testament word *imagination* simply comes from the root word *image* or "picture of the thought." Moses gave us insight as to how thoughts can turn into imaginations in this next scripture.

The Lord observed the extent of human wickedness on the earth, and he saw that everything they thought or imagined was consistently and totally evil. So the Lord was sorry he had ever

made them and put them on the earth. It broke
his heart (Genesis 6:5-6, NLT).

A few chapters later in Genesis 11, we read the story
concerning the tower of Babel. The imagination of the
people fueled the idea of building a tower to heaven. In
fact, God Himself says their imagination left uncontrolled
would be detrimental to their future.

> *And the Lord came down to see the city and the*
> *tower, which the children of men builded. And*
> *the Lord said, Behold, the people is one, and*
> *they have all one language; and this they begin*
> *to do: and now nothing will be restrained from*
> *them, which they have imagined to do* (Genesis
> 11:5-6, KJV).

I have worked with many married couples who have
experienced the heartbreak of unfaithfulness. Without
exception, the stronghold of adultery follows the same
predictable pattern. First come thoughts of being with
someone other than a spouse. If those thoughts are not
discarded, the next step of progression is always images of
being with the other person playing out in the mind. The
fantasy becomes exciting and almost real. Often this stage
will go on for weeks and months. Each time a person fan-
tasizes about being with the other person, the excitement
grows, and the consideration of painful consequences less-
ens. This is part of Satan's deception.

We are living in a sex-saturated culture. Many adver-
tisements, weekly programming, and especially movies

display sexual overtones. Various statistics abound, but it is pretty well established that a large percentage of Christian men frequently view pornography. Pornography promoters proudly declare it is victimless and try to pass it off as art and entertaining cinema. Studies prove otherwise. WebMD, a medical website, gives this warning:

> Pornography is not tough to find. Its lure is strong. Frequent use of it can be a problem personally, socially, even professionally. Some experts say heavy use of pornography can negatively affect how our brains work.[5]

The website goes on to say this:

> Experts say the same brain activity shown in drug and alcohol addiction—when circuits in your brain get associated with reward, motivation and memory get turned on—is found in those who use pornography a lot.[5]

Those who use pornography regularly have intense urges or cravings for sex. They turn to porn when they're anxious. They also tend to struggle at work and at home. Some experts believe there's an association between excessive use of porn and dissatisfaction with relationships.

The images and scenes we allow to remain in our minds have an intoxicating power in our lives. Unfortunately, I have counseled dozens of couples whose marriages have experienced challenges because the husband or wife was forced to compete with an unrealistic fantasy.

Worse yet, pornographic images are not innocent scenes you view once and never think about again. They are scenes which cause illicit feelings of excitement—both uncontrolled and ungodly. Pornography poisons your mind—it's a toxin released into your thinking.

I mentioned that years ago I, too, struggled with pornography, and I discovered something important when I started getting free from impure thinking and images. When I replaced that space with God's Word and healthy thoughts, I became smarter. Now, I know if you talk to my family and friends, they may rebut that theory, but it's true just the same. My mental ability to comprehend, remember, focus, and concentrate increased when my mind was free from the images and scenes of lust and pornography. If I would have known this years ago, I would have been a much better student in high school and college.

> Pornography poisons your mind—it's a toxin released into your thinking.

What we think, what we see, and what we listen to is food to our minds just as nutrition is to our bodies. When we allow the wrong things into our minds, it will adversely affect us. In the same way, when we fill our minds with good things, it will positively enhance us.

The same holds true in ministering to people who struggle with hopelessness to the point of inflicting harm on themselves. Thoughts of hopelessness and darkness invade their minds. If they are unable to eliminate those unhealthy thoughts or replace them with hopeful thoughts, they will begin picturing ways to bring harm to themselves to escape the pain that hounds them.

People who have intentionally harmed themselves or ended their lives entertained thoughts and images of carrying out that action. Seldom do people intentionally end their lives without confiding in someone the thoughts that continually tormented them.

The Stronghold Comes Third

If we don't take wrong thoughts captive, the thoughts will turn into images or fantasies in our minds. If we don't demolish, destroy, or forcefully rid our mind of those images and fantasies, eventually we will be under the control of a stronghold. Then once we're under the influence of a stronghold, we are imprisoned by its desires, influence, and urges. The stronghold consumes our thinking and becomes the filter through which we see and feel everything.

This is exactly what happened to Judas Iscariot. He had entertained the thoughts of wanting more money for quite a while. I am sure he even imagined various scenarios to get more money. Finally, the opportunity presented itself, and he was so consumed with the stronghold of lusting for money that he betrayed the Son of God.

Now the Feast of Unleavened Bread drew near,
which is called Passover. And the chief priests
and the scribes sought how they might kill Him,
for they feared the people. Then Satan entered

*Judas, surnamed Iscariot, who was numbered
among the twelve. So he went his way and
conferred with the chief priests and captains,
how he might betray Him to them. And they
were glad, and agreed to give him money. So
he promised and sought opportunity to betray
Him to them in the absence of the multitude*
(Luke 22:1-6).

Luke told us that "Satan entered Judas" (verse 3). The
devil did not enter Judas by force and do so against Judas'
will. Judas Iscariot was a willing participant in the scheme.

Consider again Matthew 15:19 that says, "For out of
the heart proceed evil
thoughts, murders, adul-
teries, fornications, thefts,
false witness, blasphe-
mies." What began as a
single thought turned into
the most horrible betrayal in human history.

> What began as a single thought turned into the most horrible betrayal in human history.

It seems daily we hear stories of unbelievable tragedies
and heartbreak perpetrated by friends and family members against their loved ones because of strongholds in their
lives. Drug addiction often causes people to steal from
their own families; uncontrolled jealousy and anger cause
friends to murder friends. Unchecked greed causes siblings
to steal from one another or employees to steal from a company that has been good to them.

Don't allow the devil to trick you! Satan and strongholds cannot attack you or bind you randomly without

your permission. A stronghold cannot consume you until you have repeatedly allowed your mind to move and think and focus in that direction multiple times.

You have a choice! So choose to go God's way and peace will follow.

Questions:

❶. How is the door to sin opened in our lives? And how is it closed?

❷. Does it matter what you think about? Why?

❸. What is the kingdom-of-darkness process that builds strongholds in our lives?

Prayer:

Heavenly Father, I thank You according to Your Word in James 1:5 that if we lack wisdom, we can ask of You and You will freely give us the wisdom and understanding we need. I thank You, Father, that I am gaining an understanding of how Satan schemes operate, and I will no longer be trapped by his deceptive tactics. Help me make the health of my thought a priority in my life. In Jesus' name, amen.

Chapter 7

GOD'S STRATEGY TO OVERCOME SATAN'S SCHEME

THOUGH SATAN HAS PROVEN SCHEMES THAT HAVE WREAKED HAVOC on mankind for generations, God has also given His children remarkable and potent strategies and weapons to withstand his schemes. If you will exercise these strategies, you will never have to be concerned about Satan developing a stronghold in your life. No matter what kind of thought, imagination, stronghold, or demonic scheme the devil brings along to defeat you, God has a strategy to put him in his place, which is under your feet (Ephesians 1, 2).

Through the writing of the apostle Paul, God has already detailed how to overcome each stage of Satan's scheme. Let's look at God's strategies one by one.

STRATEGY # 1: Take the Thought Captive

The easiest—and most effective—form of spiritual warfare is to take our thoughts captive. This simply means refusing to allow any ungodly, accusatory, fearful, discouraging, or condemning thoughts the right to freely roam in our minds. The apostle Paul told us all about this strategy. Look closely, once again, at this hallmark scripture on thoughts and their control:

> *Casting down imaginations, and every high thing that exalteth itself against the knowledge of God, and bringing into captivity every thought to the obedience of Christ* (2 Corinthians 10:5, KJV).

In almost every conference where I teach on the thought life, I'm asked, "How do you take your thoughts captive? What does that mean, and what does that look like?" Here's the answer: Taking thoughts captive means to recognize that a particular thought or pattern of thinking does not belong in your mind and to take intentional action to keep from entertaining those types of thoughts.

We can either take our thoughts captive, or our thoughts will take us captive.

I like to say it this way: We can either take our thoughts captive, or our thoughts will take us captive.

Earlier in my journey, I remember reading what Paul said in 2 Corinthians and thinking that he was asking the impossible. How can anyone take captive every single thought that crosses their mind? If the average person thinks between 50,000 and 60,000 thoughts a day, how can we take all those thoughts captive? Honestly, early on in my journey, my thought life was so undisciplined I was unable to intentionally stop thinking about something and intentionally start thinking about something else. I could not turn off my mind and just think about something different. So, the concept of taking every thought captive seemed unrealistic to me.

Before long, I also discovered that taking every thought captive does not only mean stopping a wrong thought but replacing it with the correct thought.

Many times, I would get out of the chair where I was sitting and walk around the room, saying to myself, "I am not going to think that. I am not going to think that." At that point, I had half of the battle won! I recognized there were thoughts that didn't belong in my mind, and I was able to chase them away for a day or so. Unfortunately, they would

> Taking every thought captive does not only mean stopping a wrong thought but replacing it with the correct thought.

always make their way back into my mind. When they did, I was back to saying, "I won't think that. I won't think that." Day after day, that scenario played out. I got momentary relief, but it did not last.

Then I saw it! It was there the whole time, and I had missed it. Look again at Philippians 4:8 below. Often in the church world, we have spent most of our time telling people what not to do instead of telling them what to do or how to do the right things. But under the inspiration of the Holy Spirit, Paul told us exactly what to spend our time thinking about.

Finally, brothers and sisters, whatever is true, whatever is noble, whatever is right, whatever is pure, whatever is lovely, whatever is admirable— if anything is excellent or praiseworthy—think about such things (Philippians 4:8, NIV).

When I saw this truth, I stopped spending my time trying not to think certain thoughts and started working on correct thoughts. Taking our thoughts captive doesn't only mean to stop thinking bad thoughts; it means to take control of our minds and think correct thoughts.

Face facts. We cannot just stop thinking. Our minds are active twenty-four hours a day, seven days a week. Our minds work even when we sleep or are unconscious. They never stop. So, it's impossible to stop thinking. The whole point is that we must direct our minds toward proper thoughts.

Then and there, I made a revolutionary change. When I caught myself thinking ungodly thoughts, I did not just say, "I am not going to think that." Instead, I said, "I take that thought captive and replace it with _____." I would find a verse of scripture that confronted the wrong thought with God's truth and filled it in the blank. There were several times while driving that I would pull off the road, get out of the car, and walk around quoting scripture to take thoughts captive and refocus my mind.

During the darkest days of my thought life battle, I would sit in a dark room for hours at a time and stare at the wall. My mind was confused, and my thoughts wouldn't turn off or focus in one direction. My wife would walk into the room and talk to me, but I wouldn't hear her. I didn't have control of my thoughts—my thoughts controlled me. But when I stopped spending my energy trying not to think certain thoughts and started spending my energy thinking the correct thoughts, things started changing.

Reading my Bible, reading faith-filled books, and listening to worship music gave me the constant ammunition I needed to aggressively take back ownership of my thought life. I also learned that reading the Bible *out loud* helped my mind to "shut up" and hear God's Word.

STRATEGY # 2:
Casting Down Imaginations with Accountability

Let's look again at 2 Corinthians 10:5 to see our second strategy. We cannot focus too much on this scripture because it's a blueprint for controlling our thought lives and walking in victory in this area.

> *Casting down imaginations, and every high thing that exalts itself against the knowledge of God, and bringing into captivity every thought*

to the obedience of Christ (2 Corinthians 10:5, KJV).

Notice the phrase *casting down* in this verse, which comes from the Greek word *kathaireo*. It means "to demolish or destroy," and it brings up an interesting point. At first, we simply learn to take our thoughts captive, but once the thoughts turn into images in our minds, we have to work hard to demolish and cast down those images. Why? Because spiritual warfare intensifies the further along the kingdom-of-darkness process advances.

To cast down gives the impression of throwing down with the intent of destroying. In other words, the mind warfare has increased to the point where we must become violent in our defense.

Numerous husbands have shared with me how they would rehearse and replay the various details of a proposed affair in their minds over and over before they built up the courage to go through with it. At first, the fear of being caught kept them from going through with the action. But the more they fantasized about it, the more the thrill overcame the fear. The fantasy locked into their minds; the images replayed over and over, igniting their flesh and physical desires.

So how do we "cast down or throw down" ungodly fantasies or imaginations? One effective way is to expose that fantasy to the light.

Satan's schemes and tactics only grow in darkness. Sin breeds in darkness—it multiplies and gains momentum in darkness. If the evil thought has advanced to an imagination or fantasy, it is one step away from consuming the person.

If you find yourself entertaining fantasies that are ungodly or impure—or if you catch yourself daydreaming continually or allowing your mind to drift off into scenes and actions which are lustful or sinful—find a trusted spiritual friend and confide in him or her. Ask the friend to pray for you and get that sinful imagination in the light.

At this point, it has progressed beyond an occasional thought that you can stop with a small amount of effort. It has now evolved into scenes that produce excitement and stir your flesh, and therefore, the warfare needed to stop this process also must intensify. That's why you need an accountability partner.

> At the imagination stage, the deception of the fantasy has become so intoxicating you cannot see the danger and downside ahead.

At the imagination stage, the deception of the fantasy has become so intoxicating you cannot see the danger and downside ahead.

> *Anyone who loves their brother and sister lives in the light, and there is nothing in them to make them stumble. But anyone who hates a brother or sister is in the darkness and walks around in the darkness. They do not know*

where they are going, because the darkness has blinded them (1 John 2:10-11, NIV).

The apostle John informed us that once we get under the influence of darkness, we are blinded or deceived. We cannot see the danger that lies ahead. If we continue down this same path without correction, the Holy Spirit will bring people or circumstances into our lives who will intercept our hypnotic fantasy with reality. The Holy Spirit understands the spiritual warfare has intensified, and if we are walking under deception, we are a lamb headed to slaughter.

An embarrassing moment, a spouse finding a text message, a friend in Christ calling us out, a planned secret phone call, or a meeting strangely interrupted are all uncomfortable scenarios and the work of the Holy Spirit shedding light on the darkness driving us. The Holy Spirit is merciful and will invade Satan's scheme with an interruption to keep us from becoming bound by a stronghold. If any of these things have happened to you, you have not simply been caught; you have been spared by a merciful heavenly Father.

For the Lord disciplines those he loves, and he punishes each one he accepts as his child. As you endure this divine discipline, remember that God is treating you as his own children. Who ever heard of a child who is never disciplined by its father? If God doesn't discipline you as he does all of his children, it means that you are

*illegitimate and are not really his children at
all. Since we respected our earthly fathers who
disciplined us, shouldn't we submit even more
to the discipline of the Father of our spirits, and
live forever? For our earthly fathers disciplined
us for a few years, doing the best they knew
how. But God's discipline is always good for us,
so that we might share in his holiness. No discipline is enjoyable while it is happening—it's
painful! But afterward there will be a peaceful
harvest of right living for those who are trained
in this way* (Hebrews 12:6-11, NLT).

Unfortunately, people sometimes won't receive their
discipline with seriousness, and they continue allowing the
fantasy to control their lives. They run past God's mercy
and the roadblocks He set up to spare them from eventual
pain and heartbreak.

For five years, I served as the district superintendent in
a region of over 220 churches and 650 ministers. Sadly, a
few times in that assignment, I had to exercise spiritual discipline upon ministers who had been unfaithful to their
spouses. In every investigation I conducted, the ministers
told of numerous times the Holy Spirit would arrest them
spiritually and emotionally or interrupt clandestine plans
they made to carry out their unfaithful actions.

The Holy Spirit was trying to rescue them from acting
on their fantasies of being with a person other than their
spouse, but they kept ignoring and running past the Lord's
roadblocks. God was trying to get that fantasy and sinful

imagination into the light because the light always disarms
Satan's schemes. The light strips away the deception of evil
intent and enables the deceived to see it for what it is—a
trap of destruction.

We are told in James 5:16, "Admit your faults to
one another and pray for each other so that you may be
healed..." (TLB). Accountability and prayer bring protection and healing. I understand that revealing to someone
about ungodly fantasies or imaginations can be embarrassing. But that moment of embarrassment is nothing
compared to the shame and pain that will be experienced
if your fantasy turns into a stronghold you act upon.

Here is another admonition for seeking out help once
we realize we are starting to come under the influence
of darkness:

> *Two can accomplish more than twice as much
> as one, for the results can be much better. If
> one falls, the other pulls him up; but if a man
> falls when he is alone, he's in trouble. Also, on
> a cold night, two under the same blanket gain
> warmth from each other, but how can one be
> warm alone? And one standing alone can
> be attacked and defeated, but two can stand
> back-to-back and conquer; three is even better,
> for a triple-braided cord is not easily broken*
> (Ecclesiastes 4:9-12, TLB).

Notice verse 12 again, which says, "...One standing
alone can be attacked and defeated, but two can stand

back-to-back and conquer." The ability to defeat the enemy is guaranteed when we do not fight alone. Two—that is a friend, a prayer partner, or an accountability partner—standing together can defeat any enemy.

My Wife, My Strong Helper

In my journey toward mental freedom, my precious wife, Amanda, became my accountability partner. As I have previously stated, my thought life was unhinged and out of control.

Being raised under strict Pentecostal tradition, there were certain things we just did not talk about, and sex was one of them. Sex was a taboo subject at church and at home. In all my years growing up in church, I never remember a Sunday school teacher, youth leader, or family member pulling me aside and talking to me about proper sexual expression, feelings, or how to harness sexual urges as a teenager or young adult.

My father and I had one talk about sex during my twenty-two years that I lived at home with my parents. That particular talk took place on my wedding day when I was twenty-two years and six months old. He told me he wanted to take me out for lunch and talk to me. I was apprehensive to say the least because he and I never had any serious man talks. He was a good, honest father, but our conversations usually only referenced the topics of sports, school, or work. We often talked about his work, which was his life, because he wanted to make sure that he instilled in me a strong work ethic, and he did.

He chose to go to Wendy's, and that was fine with me because I am a cheeseburger lover. After ordering we sat down and made small talk. The mood was a bit uncomfortable because I was waiting for him to start the serious part of this conversation. I knew he was nervous about breaching any serious subject.

Finally, he broke the ice and said, "Son, I want to talk to you about sex." If I remember correctly, I had just taken a big bite of my Wendy's double with cheese and about choked. This caught me by complete surprise. I was expecting the conversation to be about money—not going into debt buying a lot of furniture or not putting our marriage into a difficult financial position by having children too soon. But to my surprise, the subject of money never came up in the entire conversation. The last thing I expected my father to talk to me about was sex.

While chewing slowing with a mouth full of burger, I looked at him and unintelligibly muttered okay. My father then proceeded to start the infamous, father/son sex talk. But I wasn't thirteen years old. I was twenty-two.

He slowly began with these words, "Son, do you know anything about sex?"

"Yessir," I said.

"Good!" he replied. "Want a frosty?"

That was the end of the conversation.

The next words that came out of his mouth were about a new subdivision they had started in our hometown and the building materials their company was providing. The subject of sex was never again mentioned in any conversation we ever had.

So, you can see that sex was a subject I was left to explore and learn on my own. I regret to say that the high school locker room with friends was where the subject of sex was discussed most freely. My understanding of sex was formed by adolescent young men, whose values were totally different than the values around which I had been raised.

The conversations they casually talked about daily, the magazines they brought to school and passed around, and the exploits of their dating lives filled my mind with images and eventual fantasies that demanded my attention. All along, I knew the free expression of sexual gratification they so casually talked about was not proper behavior for a husband and especially for a husband who wanted to be a minister. But in my world, it was either free expression, anything and everything goes, or anything and everything was wrong. So, I struggled.

Out of fear, I was able to keep myself from acting on lustful cravings, but my thought life and fantasies included anything and everything. A daily battle of sexual thoughts, imaginations, and fantasies was followed by daily condemnation and confessing my sin to God.

By the time I became a pastor, I was a young man with a wife, a little boy, and a desire to serve God and help others but plagued by an uncontrolled thought life. This was the door that Satan used to gain entrance into my mind.

After the visitation from the Lord I received on that Saturday morning, my journey of mind renewal began. I knew the first place that had to be corrected was the lust-ful thoughts and the pornographic images and scenes I had allowed to roam freely in my mind for years. The slow, dili-gent task of taking every thought captive was difficult. My mind welcomed and used lustful thinking and fantasy as an escape from stress and weariness. Lustful images and thoughts were my default mechanism from a rough day or dealing with a situation at church where I had no answers.

As you can imagine, lust led to self-gratification, which also hindered my ability to meet the needs of my beauti-ful bride. She struggled with feelings of inadequacy and thoughts that she wasn't pleasing to me. But the truth was, during those early years she was having to compete with an unreal fantasy—something staged and not real.

As I started learning how to take back control of my thought life, I discovered early in the journey that I couldn't win this battle alone. I needed help. Being a young minister in the organization to which I was attached, there was no outlet at that time to discuss personal struggles. The con-fessing or revealing of a physical lust struggle was met with immediate dismissal, with very few opportunities for help or recovery.

With nowhere else to turn, I finally confided in Amanda. I confessed to her my daily thought battles of lust and images I saw and was unable to erase from years earlier. As a warrior prepared for battle, she forgave me and reas-sured me that together we would overcome this demonic influence. Years later, she has talked about the hurt she experienced and the feelings of emotional betrayal, but she never let on to me during my freedom journey.

At first, Amanda daily would confront me about what thoughts I had entertained during the day. "What have you been thinking about? What have you been daydreaming about?" she would ask.

Honestly, some days I didn't want to be truthful because I didn't want to hurt her. I didn't win the battle every day, and some days I was unable to take my thoughts captive. Some days were better than others, and other days were miserable failures. I'm so grateful she never gave up on me.

Slowly, very slowly, my thought life began getting renewed and healthy. Each morning as I was getting ready for work, I would read verses of scripture that Amanda had written on 3x5 postcards and taped to my bathroom mirror. As I left for work, she would hand me 3x5 cards with scriptures written on them. During the day, when lustful thoughts tried to enter my mind or I saw something that stirred my flesh, I would pull out a scripture card and begin reading it. Remember taking our thoughts captive is more than not thinking wrong thoughts. It is also replacing wrong thoughts with correct thoughts.

It has been over thirty years since those days of struggle, and even now, we continue to hold each other accountable concerning our daily thought lives. Fear, rejection, insecurity, unforgiveness, envy, the temptation to be discouraged and want to quit, plus a list a mile long of other issues can cloud our thoughts and hypnotize our minds.

Each of us needs an accountability partner to make sure we are keeping our thought lives between the lines and out of the ditch.

The words of Ecclesiastes 4:12 are so true: "One standing alone can be attacked and defeated, but two can stand back-to-back and conquer..." (TLB).

STRATEGY #3:
Using Our Weapons to Pull Down Strongholds

As believers we have the authority and knowledge to take our thoughts captive. If either through our ignorance or neglect we allow unhealthy or ungodly thoughts to remain in our thought process, those same thoughts will turn into imaginations and fantasies. Even then, the Lord is so loving and merciful that He has made a way of escaping eventual heartbreak by enabling us to cast down or throw out with force those scenes we have entertained and allowed to play and replay in our minds.

> Each of us needs an accountability partner to make sure we are keeping our thought lives between the lines and out of the ditch.

Yet if you continue to allow the darkness to control your thought life, those ungodly fantasies will eventually become so prevalent in your mind that you will begin looking for ways to act upon them. This is the point in the satanic scheme that it's no longer a thought or fantasy but a stronghold where you are driven to act upon it—you must do it; you must experience it. Only then do you realize the thrill promised and the escape offered are not the answer or the solution.

It is a prison you cannot easily escape. You find yourself a slave to an addiction or a fear. You find yourself bound by an urge or a craving never satisfied no matter how much you take, drink, or experience. It's called a stronghold, and it controls your life.

Friend, even then, God loves us so much, He has provided a way of escape. As we've read, 2 Corinthians 10:4 says, "For the weapons of our warfare are not carnal, but mighty through God to the pulling down of strong holds" (KJV).

Years ago, when I heard this verse mentioned in church, it was always preached or explained from the perspective of pulling down heavenly strongholds. This verse would always be mentioned and tied to the story in the Old Testament book of Daniel chapter 10.

Daniel had been praying and fasting for three weeks when an angel appeared informing him that his prayer had been heard but the answer had been delayed. The angel explained that the prince of the kingdom of Persia had tried to intercept the answer and keep it from getting back to earth to Daniel. The angel goes on to reveal to Daniel a scene of a heavenly battle that ensued between angels and demonic spirits.

> *And the man said to me, "Daniel, you are very precious to God, so listen carefully to what I have to say to you. Stand up, for I have been*

sent to you." When he said this to me, I stood up, still trembling. Then he said, "Don't be afraid, Daniel. Since the first day you began to pray for understanding and to humble yourself before your God, your request has been heard in heaven. I have come in answer to your prayer. But for twenty-one days the spirit prince of the kingdom of Persia blocked my way. Then Michael, one of the archangels, came to help me, and I left him there with the spirit prince of the kingdom of Persia (Daniel 10:11-13, NLT).

Putting the Old Testament verses in Daniel and the New Testament verse in 2 Corinthians 10 together, we can easily see how an understanding of strongholds in the heavenlies over cities and nations can become the focal point. Some folks took this battle to the extreme and even leased penthouse offices and apartments to hold prayer meetings. Their thought was that if they could physically get high enough, they could engage in the spiritual battle and through prayer pull down strongholds over cities and nations.

It's true that certain cities and territories have demonic influence over them that affects the attitudes and actions of the citizens of that area. But the strongholds Paul referred to in 2 Corinthians are not demonic strongholds in the heavenlies but strongholds which have developed in people's minds. The strongholds in our minds are the base of operations for people's attitudes and actions. Mental and emotional strongholds in our lives must be pulled down.

If you are reading this and realize something other than a godly influence is controlling your life, or if you are bound and imprisoned by an addiction, fear, insecurity, trauma, pornography, or some other life-controlling problem, you can be free. Remember, God has given *you* mighty spiritual weapons able to pull down the horrendous strongholds of Satan.

Paul gave us an interesting insight to this level of spiritual warfare. He told us that the stronghold must be "pulled down." In other words, the stronghold has been established in our lives and set up residence. It is controlling us at this point. It determines our actions and attitudes. It has become the number one motivation driving us. It began with a simple thought, then moved into the imagination or fantasy stage. Now the fantasy has become so intoxicating, the person will not be satisfied until he or she acts upon that fantasy.

> The strongholds in our minds are the base of operations for people's attitudes and actions.

At this point, willpower is not enough to stop this evil force. Promising never to do it again also will not be sufficient to stop this force controlling your life. You are prisoner to the urge and craving. It controls you and determines your actions and attitudes. It is a stronghold, a fortress, a prison.

The Word of God tells us it takes weapons—spiritual weapons—to pull down evil strongholds. To "pull down a stronghold" means the stronghold is evicted from its lofty position of oppressive force and control in a person's life. The stronghold controls no more, and the person is delivered!

When Paul said in 2 Corinthians 10:4 that our weapons are not carnal but mighty to pull down strongholds, he was not referring to carnal weapons—meaning guns, knives, or even educated counseling systems. Unfortunately, many people dealing with addictions have tried counseling programs that depend totally on natural methods to help. Though their motive is good, they are powerless to bring deliverance and freedom when an evil spiritual entity has entered the equation.

> To "pull down a stronghold" means the stronghold is evicted from its lofty position of oppressive force and control in a person's life.

I have worked with dozens of individuals who have attended five or six treatment centers, spent thousands of dollars, yet unfortunately they remained addicted and bound. Freedom from addictions and fears is promised through self-discipline and secular education, but the weapons to fight the spiritual evil—that is, the warden of their prison—are never discussed. In other words, these people are engaged in a spiritual battle and are only armed with natural weapons. That will never work! That would be comparable to battling a blazing house fire with a squirt gun.

When a stronghold has been set up in a person's life, it takes a power stronger than the stronghold to bring it down. If willpower was strong enough, it would have already accomplished the task or prohibited the stronghold from being established in the first place.

Look at what Luke told us:

> *But if I am casting out demons by the power of God, then the Kingdom of God has arrived among you. For when a strong man is fully armed and guards his palace, his possessions are safe— until someone even stronger attacks and overpowers him, strips him of his weapons, and carries off his belongings* (Luke 11:20-22, NLT).

I have ministered to hundreds of precious people who found themselves bound by life-controlling problems. During the entire ordeal, often lasting months and years, they promise to never give into that craving, urging, or addiction again, but unfortunately, they are powerless against its pull.

> When a stronghold has been set up in a person's life, it takes a power stronger than the stronghold to bring it down.

The Weapons Needed to Break Out of Prison

Not long after my visitation with Jesus, I began venturing out of my house. I was still somewhat apprehensive and continually fighting thoughts and harassing accusations trying to inflict me again, but I wasn't imprisoned by fear and anxiety as before.

On a Saturday morning, Amanda wanted to go to a mall in a neighboring city to shop. I agreed to accompany her. As we still do to this day, once we arrived at the mall, she went one way toward the stores, and I went the other way searching for a coffee shop or a cookie and ice cream place. Walking toward the food court, I passed by a Christian bookstore and ventured in to look around. One particular book titled *Praise Releases Faith* by Terry Law caught my eye.[6]

I had never heard of Terry Law, but the bright blue cover with the author's name in bold block font at the bottom of the book cover spiked my attention. I opened to the table of contents as I always do, and the first chapter was titled "Thought Attacks." That was all I needed to see. I quickly rushed to the counter and paid for the book. I walked just outside the bookstore and found the first bench to sit down and start reading.

The first chapter begins with a personal story Terry relays of ministering to a woman who had been in a mental institution confined by a straitjacket for a year and a half. Immediately, I remembered the sleepless nights and the images that tormented me—imaginations of me taken away to a mental institution and my wife and little boy seeing me placed in a straitjacket. That image replayed over and over in my mind with thoughts of, *You are crazy! You are losing your mind! They will come and take you away in a straitjacket!* I couldn't read fast enough at that point. I forgot all about my desire for ice cream. I had been captivated!

Terry learned from the woman's friends who brought her to the crusade service that demon entities often made her entirely unmanageable. Even that night, she suddenly became physically sick in the parking lot; evil spirits were trying to keep her from attending the service.

Let me fast forward to present day. Many times, I have heard this same story repeated. Family and friends will invite their loved ones to our meetings that minister to the emotionally and mentally bound. Before they can get their loved ones in the door, the person will get strangely ill, often outside in the parking lot on the way into the service. The devil doesn't want to give up his territory.

Terry, realizing this dear woman was under a demonic stronghold, began rebuking the evil spirit and commanding it to release its hold on the woman in Jesus' name. Apparently, the woman was being controlled by several spirits that named themselves as they left the woman. As Terry continued to minister deliverance to the woman, a spirit came out of her calling itself, "Mind Control."

As soon as that spirit left her, Terry relates that the woman's clouded eyes cleared up and focused on Terry. She smiled at him and said, "Oh, I can remember now!" That mind-control spirit had held her memory and thought processes in bondage. But the woman left that night praising God, totally delivered by the power of God.

From that experience, the author came to understand that Satan is in the business of trying to control people's minds.

> *But I fear, lest somehow, as the serpent deceived Eve by his craftiness, so your minds may be corrupted from the simplicity that is in Christ* (2 Corinthians 11:3).

The apostle Paul was aware of this satanic tactic when he wrote to the Christians at Corinth. The truth is, Satan is after our minds. He understands that if he can control our thoughts, he can direct our actions.

The devil operates in the arena of thought—your thought life is his playground.

This story reminded me of experiences I had just encountered weeks and months earlier. I couldn't remember the simplest things. My mind was clouded and tormented continually. It was like a haze covered and shrouded my mind and thoughts. I was unable to separate my thoughts logically; they ran together and never turned off. After a while, they became a continual drumbeat of confusion that captivated my consciousness.

The devil operates in the arena of thought—your thought life is his playground.

As I sat in the mall reading these first few pages, I started weeping because I finally found someone who had experience with the things I had encountered over the past few months. I read the book *Praise Releases Faith* from cover to cover several times within the next month—marking it up, highlighting, and underlining on every page. The truths in that book taught me many things, but it also served as my confirmation that I was not crazy, weak, or losing my mind. I then had a resource to help me get completely free.

Several years passed, and I kept *Praise Releases Faith* on my desk. One day I was ministering to a person who was battling with depression, and he saw the book on my desk. I had referenced the book several times in our conversation. Finally, the person asked me if he could read my book. I told him where he could buy it, and he said okay, but I could tell from his reaction that he wouldn't go to the bookstore and buy it.

He asked again, "Are you sure I can't just read your copy?" I told him the book had been a wonderful inspiration and help to my life and that I had allowed people to read other books in my library, but they were never returned. He acknowledged my reluctance and said he understood.

As we concluded and he started to walk out, I grabbed the book and made him promise he would return it after reading it. He promised, and my precious book left my possession that day for the first time in several years.

To make a long story short, two years later I tracked him down in another state. I drove to where he was and got my book. Today my copy of *Praise Releases Faith* is in a secure location in my possession. It is old, torn, and raveled at the edges, but the truths I learned about my spiritual weapons from that book continue to pull down strongholds in lives today.

Questions:

1. What are the three God-given strategies that will enable you to withstand the devil's schemes?

2. Why is an accountability partner important when dealing with addictions, fears, lusts, pornography, etc.? Do you have an accountability partner? What things would be good for you to discuss with him or her?

3. How do strongholds affect a person's attitudes and actions? How might strongholds affect you?

Prayer:

Heavenly Father, I thank You according to Your Word in Isaiah 54:17 that no weapon formed against me will prosper. Help me be diligent in guarding my thought life and prohibiting ungodly and unhealthy thoughts and images in my mind. I recognize I also need accountability in my life and welcome accountability through trusted friends whom you send into my life. In Jesus' name, amen.

Chapter 8

A MIGHTY ARSENAL OF WEAPONRY

EOPLE OFTEN CONTACT ME AFTER HEARING MY STORY. HEARING everything I went through and how the Lord set me free gives them hope that they can find freedom as well. Without question, freedom is available to all—though it comes with a fight. But it is a fight we're definitely not in alone. As children of God, we have mighty supernatural weapons so formidable they can demolish any stronghold of Satan. This is fantastic news and a truth we must boldly believe and declare. We can rejoice that no one is beyond God's help—no one. Our victory is all about learning to wield the mighty weaponry God has given us.

The very nature of the word *stronghold,* which Paul talks about in 2 Corinthians 10, lets us know that effort and determination have been exerted against us to imprison us. Likewise, it will take effort and determination to get free from this prison. The effort and determination I refer to is not physical strength or willpower but the diligence to use our spiritual weapons to walk in liberty, even more than the devil has been diligent to harass and imprison us.

Every day all day, my mind was bombarded with thoughts of quitting, giving in, and giving up. Many times, I entertained thoughts of ending my life because the promises in God's Word of peace and a sound mind seemed so far removed from the reality I was facing. But I resolved that I would not give up or give in.

I remember walking through my house shouting at the tormenting thoughts blaring in my mind. I recall the thoughts and images of the police and medical professionals coming to get me and forcefully taking me to a facility for the mentally insane. But even with those scenes playing out in my mind, I would yell, "I don't care if they take me away, I will never surrender to these thoughts. I will continually declare that God has given me a sound mind."

It was a fight—a constant warfare—for over a year. But I continued to use my spiritual weapons—weapons mighty through God to the pulling down of strongholds. And those weapons, which I am detailing in this book, are the spiritual weapons that eventually set me free. They are the weapons that will set you free—and keep you free!

WEAPON #1—The Word of God

Your Bible is your weapon—it's the number one weapon in your arsenal.

For the word of God is alive and powerful. It is sharper than the sharpest two-edged sword, cutting between soul and spirit, between joint and marrow. It exposes our innermost thoughts and desires (Hebrews 4:12, NLT).

This verse tells us that our Bible is not just any book. It is not just paper and ink. It is a weapon that is alive and powerful, and its purpose is to help you protect, defend, and obtain. It will protect and defend you and your family. It will help you obtain everything God has promised you so that you can live an abundant life.

The apostle Peter, under the inspiration of the Holy Spirit, gave us amazing insight into the power contained in our Bible. Peter told us that the truth in our Bible has the power to give us the very life of God.

This letter is from Simon Peter, a slave and apostle of Jesus Christ. I am writing to you who share the same precious faith we have. This faith was given to you because of the justice and fairness of Jesus Christ, our God and Savior. May God give you more and more grace and peace as you grow in your knowledge of God and Jesus our Lord. By his divine power, God has given us everything we need for living a godly life. We have received all of this by coming to know him, the one who called us to himself by means of his marvelous glory and excellence. And because of his glory and excellence, he has given us great

*and precious promises. These are the promises
that enable you to share his divine nature and
escape the world's corruption caused by human
desires* (2 Peter 1:1-4, NLT).

Unfortunately, many people's devil-defeating, life-giving, spiritual weapon—the Bible—sits unused on a desk or shelf. Too often it's a weapon the possessor doesn't know how to use.

Recently I was visiting with a family and the conversation turned toward the possibility of someone breaking into their house to rob and injure them.

I asked them, "Don't you have a gun?"

"Yes, we have a gun," the homeowner replied. "But I'd have to ask the intruder to show me how to use it because I don't know how to load it or fire it."

It doesn't seem logical or smart to possess a weapon without knowing how to use that weapon. Yet, many Christians are in the same condition. Satan is the thief who comes to steal from us and destroy our families, but we have a formidable weapon available to defeat him. The words in our Bible are powerful enough to render him ineffective, but too many believers don't know how to use them.

> The power of our Bible is contained in our faith and confidence in what it says.

The power of our Bible is contained in our faith and confidence in what it says. When we don't know what it says, our Bible is useless even though it carries the power of life and death. This is the reason so many Christians are powerless and being defeated by our enemy.

I discovered years ago that my love for God should run parallel to my love for the Word of God. In other words, I don't love God any more than I love His Word.

The Word or Good Feelings

The Pentecostal, Charismatic style of worship is often filled with emotional celebrations and intense seasons of intercession. It's not uncommon in one of these services to see dancing, joyful singing, and at the same time, a heartfelt cry of repentance. Often the emotional response felt in a service becomes the focal point of the service and the confirmation to the participants that God has been in their presence.

I was born and raised in a Pentecostal Church, a church that believes the Bible is God's Word. But God's Word didn't have first place in my life—good emotional feelings did. Ask yourself the same question. Which has first place in your life?

My Holy Spirit moment was different than many of the young people in our little church. Whereas many of the kids in our youth group received the Holy Spirit at a youth service or youth camp, I received the infilling of the Holy Spirit in a private time of prayer.

One Sunday night, the pastor preached on the subject "Tarry Until" with the emphasis on "tarrying for the Holy Ghost." The premise was that the disciples had to wait for the Holy Spirit to fall on the day of Pentecost in Acts 2, so we must be willing to wait also. The altar call was given to tarry or wait for the Holy Ghost, so I responded. I remember thinking, *Hopefully, we won't have to wait for days like the disciples did in the book of Acts because I have to go to school the next day.*

Anytime the youth went forward to the altar in our small Pentecostal church, the older ladies would gather around and start praying for them. The goal was to get all the youth filled with the Holy Ghost and speaking in tongues.

While kneeling at the altar, suddenly I found myself surrounded by the "mothers of Israel," as I called them. One of them grabbed one of my arms and raised it while another grabbed my other arm and held it up. Thus, the altar service ramped up to full speed.

My mother was playing the organ, and the church ladies had me surrounded. A few other young people knelt at other places around the front, but it appeared that night I was the selected Holy Ghost target. A combination of praises, hallelujahs, and various ladies switching back and forth from tongues to English in my ear kept my attention captivated. I remember one on my right side, saying, "Let go, son!" Another on my left side was saying, "Hold on, son!"

Now if you have never been a part of an old-fashioned Pentecostal altar service, you have not experienced real church. Time is not considered, and quietness is a sign of spiritual coldness. The voices were praying loudly, the music was a victory march, and the ebb and flow of the altar service would shift and swoon with the intensity of the next mother who would take the prayer lead.

I don't know how long we stayed at the altar that night, but it was long enough that I had become weary of praying and calling on God at the top of my lungs. This "tarrying until" was becoming more than I bargained for. My shirt was soaked with sweat, and my arms were numb from being held up. Finally, I gasped out a mumbled breath from weariness, and when I did, one of the ladies hollered, "You got it! You got it!"

Suddenly the mood switched from "pressing in" to celebration. People starting clapping and rejoicing accompanied with cheers of "Thank You, Jesus!" from everyone around the altar. The ladies were excited because they thought they had prayed another child through to the Holy Ghost.

After being hugged and squeezed by every grandmother in the church and patted on the back by every man, people started making their way back to their seats to retrieve their possessions and head home. Another young person Holy-Ghost-filled, another altar service enjoyed where God came down and glory filled their souls.

As we walked through the door out to the parking lot, I remember a woman saying, "Son, I am so glad you got it!"

I remembered politely and quietly saying, "Thank you." But as I walked away, I remember thinking, *If this is the infilling of the Holy Spirit, this is the no nearest nothing I have ever experienced.*

I didn't sleep much that night. I was disappointed. I experienced a lot of emotions around the altar, but there was no substance that occurred in my heart. I was under the impression that the infilling of the Holy Spirit was to empower a person with spiritual power. I read about the disciple's lives being changed after their experience on the day of Pentecost. I read where men filled with fear immediately turned into men of boldness. If a spiritual power came, surely I would know it and sense a change. But unfortunately, none of that happened to me that night.

The next day at school I kept replaying the scene from Sunday night, questioning what I had experienced. When I got home, I went to my room and started reading my Bible, looking for answers. I knew God was real and believed what the Bible said was true, but what I had experienced was disappointing because I didn't sense any change in my heart at all.

Two years earlier, I had responded to an altar call at a summer revival meeting, and the moment I prayed and asked Jesus to come into my life, I knew inside that a transformation had taken place. I knew I was different.

By Tuesday night, I had looked up all the Holy Spirit scriptures I could find in my Bible. I desired to experience what the disciples experienced in Jerusalem that momentous day, but I didn't want to go through another emotional roller coaster with all those people at church. I was about to close my Bible and stop reading for the night when I stumbled upon an important scripture.

*And so I tell you, keep on asking, and you will
receive what you ask for. Keep on seeking, and
you will find. Keep on knocking, and the door
will be opened to you. For everyone who asks,
receives. Everyone who seeks, finds. And to
everyone who knocks, the door will be opened.
You fathers—if your children ask for a fish, do
you give them a snake instead? Or if they ask
for an egg, do you give them a scorpion? Of
course not! So if you sinful people know how to
give good gifts to your children, how much more
will your heavenly Father give the Holy Spirit
to those who ask him* (Luke 11:9-13, NLT).

As a twelve-year-old boy, it was as if a light from heaven
immediately shined in my heart. Suddenly, I saw it! I didn't
need to do emotional cartwheels to receive the Holy Ghost,
and I didn't have to tarry for a long time. I simply had to
ask the heavenly Father, and He would give me the infilling of the Holy Spirit.

"...How much more will your heavenly Father give the
Holy Spirit to those who ask him," I just read. I fell asleep
that night with a peace in my heart and a plan to receive
the Holy Spirit. In fact, the next day was Wednesday and
church Bible study, so I planned to ask the heavenly Father
then for the baptism of the Holy Spirit.

Normally on Wednesday night, I would take my
schoolwork to church with me and do homework while
my grandfather taught the lesson. But on that night, the
only thing I took to church was my Bible. I don't remember

what my grandfather's Bible study was about. I was looking forward to the prayer time at the end of service.

When I was a child, at the end of every service in our church, everyone would be invited to come to the front and find a place to spend a few moments in personal prayer before they left the church house. We must be prayed up before we go out into a sin-cursed world. This night was no exception. My grandfather finished his lesson and "opened the altars for prayer," which meant an invitation was extended for people to come forward to pray. There were probably only twenty-five or thirty people in that service, so the altar area wasn't crowded. But I wasn't getting anywhere close to the altar that night. What happened last time was nothing short of a Holy Ghost gang up, and I wasn't allowing those grannies to get a hold of me again.

I waited till everyone had gone up to the front to pray and slipped out of my pew. I walked down toward the front but turned into an empty pew about four rows from the front. I knelt down and opened my Bible to Luke 11:13, "So if you sinful people know how to give good gifts to your children, how much more will your heavenly Father give the Holy Spirit to those who ask him" (NLT).

I remember saying softly, "Lord, You said right here that if I would ask You for the Holy Spirit, You would give Him to me. So, I ask You to fill me with the Holy Spirit now."

Without hollering or marching music—even without raised arms—there, kneeling alone, a sense of joy immediately rose up inside of me. I didn't know how to respond or what to say except, "Thank You, Jesus." In a moment's time, that intelligible "thank you" turned into a language I had never heard, spoken, or learned. At first, I was so shocked by what I heard myself saying that I stopped and made sure I wasn't dreaming. Then like a river that had been released, I opened my mouth and yielded my heart. Words flowed out in a language that I had never heard before. With each moment that passed, my heart became more excited and freer. I sensed freshness, newness, and life.

An excitement took over my emotions, and I began to cry out of joy. Once my crying started, I calmed myself the best I could because I didn't want the grandmothers to hear me and take that as a sign to give me a Pentecostal double dose.

I don't know how long I knelt there, but it must have been a while because when I stood up and looked around, everybody was already back in their seats and looking at me. I slowly made my way back to my regular pew and sat down. Maybe I should say that I floated back to my regular pew and sat down. I was on cloud nine. This was it!

The next several months was totally different for me. I wanted to witness to all my friends and share what had happened to me. Most of them thought I was crazy, but I didn't care. I got it, and it was real!

For months I lived in an emotional euphoria. At every church service, I couldn't hold back the tears. They were not tears of sadness; I had an unusual joy and thankfulness in my heart. Every song stirred my heart, and every sermon inspired me. I loved going to church and couldn't wait to get there.

Yet, over a period of time, I came to rely upon those emotional feelings. I assessed the move of the Holy Spirit by the emotional response I witnessed or experienced. If there were emotions of crying, that meant there was repentance. If there were emotions of joy, that meant the Holy Spirit had come down. If the service really got carried away and the preacher didn't get to preach because people were laughing, dancing, or falling under the power of the Spirit, then that was the epitome of a Holy Ghost-filled service. The preaching of the Word of God was important, but a good sermon would always take an inferior position to a Holy Ghost move.

At the same time, I began noticing it was always the same folks going to the altar for prayer in every service. It seemed like people were going to the altar, but their lives were not being altered.

Also, in the New Testament books of Acts, when the disciples were filled with the Holy Spirit, they began witnessing. Their witness and testimony of what Jesus had done for them compelled others to come and see what was taking place. But new folks were not coming into our church; no one invited anybody. A great church service was not the result of people being born again but what kind of experience the regular crowd had around the altar.

Later that year, my grandfather resigned as pastor of the church after serving for twenty-two years. I had never been to a church where my grandfather was not the pastor, so things started changing quickly. Within a few weeks, new preachers started coming in every Sunday. One Sunday a young couple came and preached. I don't remember their names, and I never saw them after that particular Sunday. Yet almost fifty years later, I still remember he preached a sermon titled, "The Power of the Word of God."

I listened intently as he talked about things I had never heard before. He talked about using the Word of God every day in your life. I was under the impression that the Bible was for Sundays and the stories in the Bible were for preachers to preach messages. *I had the Holy Ghost, so why did I need to study the Bible every day? Every Sunday and Wednesday I can get filled up with the Holy Ghost, and that is all I need,* I reasoned.

For years, I believed that the Holy Ghost was all I needed. I graduated college with a bachelor's degree in religion. Many of my studies were about the historical accuracy of the Bible. I studied the Greek language and took Hebrew classes. Each class was taught about the Bible, but none of them taught me how to apply the Bible to my daily life. That didn't concern me then because I had the Holy Ghost. I had the "fantastic feeling."

But years later, while driving down the road, that rogue thought popped into my mind: *You must be demon possessed.* Suddenly, the fantastic feeling left, and no matter how much I prayed and cried, I could not get that feeling back.

Praying and crying also did not make the harassing thoughts stop. I prayed more during that year than any time in my life. Before fear grabbed me and held me a prisoner in my home, I would get around the altar every day at our little church and cry for hours pouring out my heart to God. I was trying to get that feeling back and trying to chase the harassment away, but it was not working.

God's Word Alive and Powerful

The prophet said it well in Hosea 4:6, "My people are destroyed for lack of knowledge." I didn't understand that my Bible is a powerful weapon. As long as I was blinded to the revelation of the power in God's Word, Satan kept me in defeat.

> As long as I was blinded to the revelation of the power in God's Word, Satan kept me in defeat.

Today we have numerous Christians who think they have an understanding about God and His ways, but their thinking does not line up with the Bible. It's impossible to know the ways of God if we are not students of His Word.

Let's look again at Hebrews 4:

> *For the word of God is alive and powerful. It is sharper than the sharpest two-edged sword, cutting between soul and spirit, between joint and marrow. It exposes our innermost thoughts and desires* (Hebrews 4:12, NLT).

The writer of Hebrews informs us that the Word is alive and powerful. The Greek language translates *word* as *logos*. In this verse, it is referring to the written Word of God, our Bible.

Then we see the same Greek word *logos* is used in the gospel of John:

> *In the beginning the Word already existed. The Word was with God, and the Word was God. He existed in the beginning with God. God created everything through him, and nothing was created except through him. The Word gave life to everything that was created, and his life brought light to everyone. The light shines in the darkness, and the darkness can never extinguish it* (John 1:1-5, NLT).

In these verses, the Greek word *logos* is not referring to the written Word of God, the Bible, but to the Living Word of God, Jesus. I often hear people say, "Oh, I wished I had lived when Jesus was alive to see all the things He did and experience the healings and miracles He performed. Things would be much better today if Jesus were here."

The truth is, Jesus is the living Word, but we have the written Word. It wasn't Jesus the human who was powerful but Jesus the Word of God who was powerful. We have the Word of God that the New Testament citizens had, just in a different form. But the power has not diminished.

Both the written Word of God and the living Word of God contain the Life of God.

*The Word gave life to everything that was cre-
ated, and his life brought light to everyone
(John 1:4, NLT).*

The word *life* is the Greek word *zoe,* which means "life
as God has it." Jesus gave the God-kind of life to everything
He encountered and brought the God-kind of life to us.

You'll recall that in Hebrews 4:12 it says, "The word of
God is *alive and powerful*" (NLT). The word *alive* in the
original language is a compound of two Greek words *zoe*
(life as God has it) and *poieo*
(to make). In other words,
Jesus is the living Word
come to give life. The Bible,
the written Word—when
we believe and act upon it—
will make us alive with the
life of God. Our Bible, the Word of God, is a weapon that
furnishes the same power Jesus had when He walked on
earth, but we must believe and act upon it.

> The Word of God is a weapon
> that furnishes the same
> power Jesus had when He
> walked on earth, but we must
> believe it and act upon it.

Time and time again, we read instances in the New
Testament when people believed and acted upon the Word
of God, and God's power was manifested.

*When Jesus returned to Capernaum, a Roman
officer came and pleaded with him, "Lord,
my young servant lies in bed, paralyzed and
in terrible pain." Jesus said, "I will come and
heal him." But the officer said, "Lord, I am
not worthy to have you come into my home.*

Just say the word from where you are, and my servant will be healed. I know this because I am under the authority of my superior officers, and I have authority over my soldiers. I only need to say, 'Go,' and they go, or 'Come,' and they come. And if I say to my slaves, 'Do this,' they do it." When Jesus heard this, he was amazed. Turning to those who were following him, he said, "I tell you the truth, I haven't seen faith like this in all Israel! And I tell you this, that many Gentiles will come from all over the world—from east and west—and sit down with Abraham, Isaac, and Jacob at the feast in the Kingdom of Heaven. But many Israelites—those for whom the Kingdom was prepared—will be thrown into outer darkness, where there will be weeping and gnashing of teeth." Then Jesus said to the Roman officer, "Go back home. Because you believed, it has happened." And the young servant was healed that same hour (Matthew 8:5-13, NLT).

Here is an example of a man who had the same faith in the Word of God as he had in Jesus the Living Word of God. The Roman officer goes to Jesus to tell Him about his servant who was paralyzed and in severe pain. Jesus said to the Roman officer that He would personally go and heal the servant. How did the officer respond? He said, "You don't have to come personally. Just speak the word, and my servant will be healed." In other words, the Roman officer believed the Word of God carried the same power and ability as Jesus carried in the flesh.

If we have the same faith in God's Word as we would in Jesus personally coming to do something for us, we will see the exact same results.

The truth that equipped me to pull down the stronghold of fear, lust, and condemnation that had been established in my mind was this: The supernatural power of God resident in Jesus—the living Word of God—is also contained in the Bible—the written Word of God.

> The supernatural power of God resident in Jesus—the living Word of God—is also contained in the Bible—the written Word of God.

I realized my Bible wasn't just a historical book, and it wasn't simply a sacred text. Its words contain the life and power of God.

When that simple truth dawned on me, the verses below took on new meaning in my life.

> *But if you remain in me and my words remain in you, you may ask for anything you want, and it will be granted! When you produce much fruit, you are my true disciples. This brings great glory to my Father* (John 15:7-8, NLT).

Jesus tells us that when the Word of God becomes a part of our lives and the Bible gets in us, then our requests are motivated and activated by God's Word that is alive and powerful.

Angels respond to His Word, demonic spirits respond to His Word, sickness and disease respond to His Word, and the environment responds to His Word.

Jesus and His Word carry the same power—it's the container that is the difference. The powerful life-giving Word of God was contained in Jesus' flesh body when He was alive on earth. Today, the Bible contains the life-giving, powerful Word of God, and we must believe it and act upon it, which is called faith.

My love, honor, and respect of God's Word must coincide with my love, honor, and respect of Jesus. It's interesting that people easily believe in the historical Jesus and the power He displayed when He walked planet Earth, but they struggle believing that same power of God is available today through believing and acting on His Word.

Many view the Bible as a history book that teaches us how to live based on other people's actions and life events. The Bible is a wonderful book of lessons and a supreme teacher, but it is also much more than that. The Bible is the life and power of God to those who believe and act upon it.

> *For I am not ashamed of this Good News about Christ. It is the power of God at work, saving everyone who believes—the Jew first and also the Gentile* (Romans 1:16, NLT).

Paul said the Bible is the power, the *dunamis* (Greek), the ability and might of God. He continued to say it is the power and ability of God at work toward everyone who believes.

This was the key that I missed growing up in church. I believed in Jesus and was born again. I was filled with the Spirit and spoke in tongues. I even preached sermons and used the Bible as my resource. And that's my point: My Bible was a resource to me—not a life source. When my Bible became my life source, the power of God was released in my life, and my Bible became a mighty weapon.

Acting on the Word

I have asked the Lord to give me the ability to articulate in writing the efficacy of encouraging you to believe and act upon the written Word of God. I encourage you to believe and act upon what Jesus said in the Bible as if He appeared to you and said it in person.

After Jesus appeared to me, the demonic spirits didn't cease their attack against my mind. For a short season, the thought attacks diminished, but they came back. Jesus didn't reappear to me each time the thought attacks came back. No, I had to do something about it. I had to resist and withstand those thought attacks, and the way I remained free was to believe, confess, and act on the Word of God.

> When my Bible became my life source, the power of God was released in my life, and my Bible became a mighty weapon.

The dumb devil took advantage of my lack of understanding for months and years. It wasn't a fair fight. He knew things I did not know and imprisoned me because of my ignorance.

But when he came back around to imprison me again with those same fearful, condemning thoughts, the fight once again was not fair. This time it was a lopsided fight in my favor.

Those harassing thoughts that once tormented me with fear and paranoia lost their power and sting when I responded with the Word of God. Every tactic, thought, scene, memory, and imagination Satan previously used successfully against me was rendered powerless by the Word of God that I confessed and meditated on daily.

Remember, the key is not owning a Bible, reading it periodically, or even knowing the Bible well. The Bible only turns into a weapon and a defense in our lives when we believe it and do what it says.

> *Anyone who listens to my teaching and follows it is wise, like a person who builds a house on solid rock. Though the rain comes in torrents and the floodwaters rise and the winds beat against that house, it won't collapse because it is built on bedrock. But anyone who hears my teaching and doesn't obey it is foolish, like a person who builds a house on sand. When the rains and floods come and the winds beat against that house, it will collapse with a mighty crash"* (Matthew 7:24-27, NLT).

Jesus tells us that Christians can be destroyed and swept away into mental defeat and emotional discouragement. In no way does being a Christian make us immune from mental or emotional storms. But in Matthew 7, Jesus informed us that although the storms rage and the attacks come, those who withstand and endure the onslaught of Satan are those who do what the Word of God says. Just hearing the Bible preached on Sunday is not enough. We must act upon it and obey it.

The Word of God became the all-consuming, driving force in my life. I read the Bible daily and memorized it continually. When thoughts of defeat and discouragement tried to enter my mind, I refused to entertain them. Instead, I quoted a Bible verse I had memorized. Sometimes I had to quote verses multiple times because harassing thoughts wouldn't immediately stop.

Scriptures to Memorize

Let me encourage you to memorize the following verses from your Bible. These are the verses I used, which instilled in me a confidence in the power of God's Word. I read and quoted these verses daily until they became a part of my very being.

> HEBREWS 4:12 (NLT)—*For the word of God is alive and powerful. It is sharper than the sharpest two-edged sword, cutting between soul and spirit, between joint and marrow. It exposes our innermost thoughts and desires.*

> MATTHEW 24:35 (NLT)—*Heaven and earth will disappear, but my words will never disappear.*

LUKE 4:32—*And they were astonished at His teaching, for His word was with authority.*

JOHN 6:63—*It is the Spirit who gives life; the flesh profits nothing. The words that I speak to you are spirit, and they are life.*

JOHN 14:24—*He who does not love Me does not keep My words; and the word which you hear is not Mine but the Father's who sent Me.*

JOHN 8:51—*Most assuredly, I say to you, if anyone keeps My word, he shall never see death.*

JOHN 14:23—*Jesus answered and said to him, "If anyone loves Me, he will keep My word; and My Father will love him, and We will come to him and make Our home with him."*

1 JOHN 2:3—*Now by this we know that we know Him, if we keep His commandments.*

PSALM 119:89 (NLT)—*Your eternal word, O Lord, stands firm in heaven.*

ISAIAH 40:8 (NLT)—*The grass withers and the flowers fade, but the word of our God stands forever.*

1 PETER 1:25 (NLT)—*But the word of the Lord remains forever. And that word is the Good News that was preached to you.*

JEREMIAH 15:16 (NLT)—*When I discovered your words, I devoured them. They are my joy and my heart's delight, for I bear your name, O Lord God of Heaven's Armies.*

2 TIMOTHY 3:16 (NLT)—*All Scripture is inspired by God and is useful to teach us what is true and to make us realize what is wrong in our lives. It corrects us when we are wrong and teaches us to do what is right.*

PSALM 119:11 (NLT)—*I have hidden your word in my heart, that I might not sin against you.*

COLOSSIANS 3:16—*Let the word of Christ dwell in you richly in all wisdom, teaching and admonishing one another in psalms and hymns and spiritual songs, singing with grace in your hearts to the Lord.*

PSALM 19:8 (NLT)—*The commandments of the Lord are right, bringing joy to the heart. The commands of the Lord are clear, giving insight for living.*

PSALM 119:105 (NLT)—*Your word is a lamp to guide my feet and a light for my path.*

2 PETER 1:18-19 (PHILLIPS)—*We actually heard that voice speaking from Heaven while we were with him on the sacred mountain. The*

*word of prophecy was fulfilled in our hearing!
You should give that word your closest attention, for it shines like a lamp amidst all the dirt
and darkness of the world, until the day dawns,
and the morning star rises in your hearts.*

PSALM 119:97 (NLT)—*Oh, how I love your
instructions! I think about them all day long.*

PSALM 33:4 (NLT)—*For the word of the
Lord holds true, and we can trust everything
he does.*

PSALM 107:20 (NIV)—*He sent out his word
and healed them; he rescued them from the
grave.*

PSALM 119:77 (NLT)—*Surround me with
your tender mercies so I may live, for your
instructions are my delight.*

PSALM 119:145-148 (NLT)—*I pray with all
my heart; answer me, Lord! I will obey your
decrees. I cry out to you; rescue me, that I may
obey your laws. I rise early, before the sun is
up; I cry out for help and put my hope in your
words. I stay awake through the night, thinking about your promise.*

Each of these verses helped me see the importance of
God's Word while I was fighting for my mental life.

Let me encourage you to reread the final passage above from Psalm 119:145-148, written by David, and envision the despair he experienced and the hope he expected. As I read these verses, I was able to relate to King David. While I was going through mental and emotional hell, I prayed with all my heart and cried out to God for rescue with every fiber of my being. Day after day, I watched the sun rise, crying for God's help to make it through another day. The nights were the worst, as the thoughts of fear and images of death invaded my mind like a flood. I could relate to the hopelessness David was feeling.

But then I noticed David didn't stop with his despair or hopelessness. David had one goal through all his pain—to believe in and obey God's Word. Obeying God's Word was David's hope. It was his rescue, and it was his deliverance.

Years later now, I am writing to you because the Word of God I committed to memory and deposited in my heart eventually rescued me from the mental onslaught of Satan. The personal visitations I had from the Lord helped me greatly, but it was the Word of the Lord—my Bible I embraced daily—that has kept me free for many years. God's Word will do the same for you!

Here are a few other verses that played a significant role in my life. These verses instilled in me an understanding of the power in God's Word and the need to have it abiding in me. As these verses became my life source, thoughts of fear and condemnation that had dominated me for years lost their grip on my mind and life.

EPHESIANS 1:17-23—*that the God of our Lord Jesus Christ, the Father of glory, may give to you the spirit of wisdom and revelation in the knowledge of Him, the eyes of your understanding being enlightened; that you may know what is the hope of His calling, what are the riches of the glory of His inheritance in the saints, and what is the exceeding greatness of His power toward us who believe, according to the working of His mighty power which He worked in Christ when He raised Him from the dead and seated Him at His right hand in the heavenly places, far above all principality and power and might and dominion, and every name that is named, not only in this age but also in that which is to come. And He put all things under His feet and gave Him to be head over all things to the church, which is His body, the fullness of Him who fills all in all.*

EPHESIANS 3:14-20—*For this reason I bow my knees to the Father of our Lord Jesus Christ, from whom the whole family in heaven and earth is named, that He would grant you, according to the riches of His glory, to be strengthened with might through His Spirit in the inner man, that Christ may dwell in your hearts through faith; that you, being rooted and grounded in love, may be able to comprehend with all the saints what is the width and length and depth and height— to know the love of Christ which passes knowledge; that you may be filled with all the fullness of God. Now to Him who is able to do exceedingly abundantly above all that we ask or think, according to the power that works in us.*

PROVERBS 30:5 (NLT)—*Every word of God proves true. He is a shield to all who come to him for protection.*

ECCLESIASTES 8:4—*Where the word of a king is, there is power....*

EPHESIANS 6:17 (NLT)—*Put on salvation as your helmet, and take the sword of the Spirit, which is the word of God.*

1 THESSALONIANS 2:13 (NLT)—*Therefore, we never stop thanking God that when you received his message from us, you didn't think of our words as mere human ideas. You accepted what we said as the very word of God—which, of course, it is. And this word continues to work in you who believe.*

JAMES 1:21 (NLT)—*So get rid of all the filth and evil in your lives, and humbly accept the word God has planted in your hearts, for it has the power to save your souls.*

I memorized these verses many years ago in my darkest hours. Yet these same verses rise up in me today when thought attacks try to distract me and captivate my mind.

Sow Today, Reap Tomorrow

Some years ago, sitting in the Houston airport catching a connecting flight to Tulsa, Oklahoma, I saw Pastor John and Dodie Osteen walking down the corridor. He was the pastor of the great Lakewood Church in Houston and the father of noted author Joel Osteen. I punched Amanda and said, "Look, there is Pastor John and Dodie Osteen." I watched him on television every Sunday night. In my eyes he was the premier pastor of pastors. He was a man of faith, passion, and integrity. He was bigger than life to me and a man I admired and longed to meet one day.

I couldn't take my eyes off of him as they came closer. Amanda and I were flying commercial airlines and waiting at the gate for our flight to board. I told Amanda that I bet they were walking down to a gate where people keep their private jets. But to my surprise, they slowed their pace and turned into the gate area where we were sitting and sat down across from us. I couldn't believe it. The world-renowned John Osteen was flying on the same plane as me. I tried not to stare, but I couldn't help it.

After a few minutes, I guess he saw me struggling not to stare, and he smiled at me. I felt embarrassed and smiled back and ducked my head.

Amanda said, "This is your chance! Walk over and meet him and tell him how much you appreciate his ministry."

"But I don't want to bother him," I responded.

"This is the best chance you will ever have," she replied.

A couple minutes more and I worked up the courage to walk over and introduce myself. I told him how much I loved his ministry and how I watched him every Sunday night in Tennessee. To my amazement, he asked me to sit down beside him, and he asked me about my church and my life. For the next fifteen minutes, I was in heaven, listening to every word he shared.

Our conversation was stopped when the desk attendant called for the flight to start boarding. I shook his hand and once again told him that I appreciated his ministry and was so thankful to meet him. We boarded the plane, and since we were not the first one hundred passengers seated, we had to take available seats toward the rear of the plane. As the plane took off, I was reflecting on my conversation with Pastor Osteen. I had even started writing down some notes of the things he shared because I didn't want to forget them.

The plane reached our cruising altitude, and the pilot came on the intercom telling the passengers they could move around the cabin if needed. A minute or two later, I glanced up and noticed Pastor Osteen walking down the aisle toward the back of the plane where we were seated.

I punched Amanda and said, "Look, here comes Pastor Osteen! I bet he is going to the bathroom."

"Eddie, most people have to go to the restroom at some time during the day," she answered me, laughing. When I realized how silly my comment was and how starstruck I had become, we both had a good chuckle.

As he got closer to where we were sitting, instead of walking past us, he stopped at our aisle and said, "Eddie, do you have a few more minutes to talk?"

I was stunned and just shook my head yes.

"Squeeze over!" Pastor Osteen said and sat down on the arm rest of my aisle seat. For the next five to ten minutes, he began sharing with me some things about ministry. Those few things he talked about still resonate in my heart and mind many years later.

> The memorization of scripture has been the greatest weapon I have discovered to combat anxiety attacks, runaway thoughts, and the harassment of my mind by fear and doubt.

He told me one thing in particular that I have never forgotten. I think about it continually because I have discovered it to be true over and over. He said, "Eddie, if you will put God's Word in your heart when you don't need it, the Holy Spirit will be faithful to bring it out of your heart when you do need it."

Pastor Osteen has since stepped over to heaven, but that day on the plane he told me a truth that has helped me immensely through the years. The memorization of scripture has been the greatest weapon I have discovered to combat anxiety attacks, runaway thoughts, and the harassment of my mind by fear and doubt.

On the good days when my mind was not under attack, I learned to commit a portion of my daily devotion to scripture memorization. I would take time and memorize one verse per week. It didn't take much effort, but the benefits to my life were immense.

Amazingly, it never failed. On the tough days, when anxiety would try to invade my mind and fear would try to flood my thinking, the Holy Spirit would always bring up a verse I had memorized. That memorized verse was like a sword that rose up in me and cut through the deception and fear the devil tried to inflict upon me.

> *In addition to all of these, hold up the shield of faith to stop the fiery arrows of the devil. Put on salvation as your helmet, and take the sword of the Spirit, which is the word of God* (Ephesians 6:16-17, NLT).

Once your Bible, the very word of God, becomes your life force deposited in your heart and mind, it will become a weapon of power that destroys anxiety, fear, and every tactic of Satan.

Satan Hates to be Ignored

During the season I struggled with relentless thought attacks, I learned how resistance is most effective against Satan. Look with me at a wonderful verse, known by most Christians, that promises this very thing.

So humble yourselves before God. Resist the devil, and he will flee from you (James 4:7, NLT).

According to Vine's Dictionary, the word *resist* in the original Greek is *antitasso*. The word has many variances of meanings, depending on which form of the word is used. One form means "to oppose or rage in battle against." It carries the idea of aggressive behavior.[7]

...After Silas and Timothy came down from Macedonia, Paul spent all his time preaching the word. He testified to the Jews that Jesus was the Messiah. But when they opposed and insulted him, Paul shook the dust from his clothes and said, "Your blood is upon your own heads—I am innocent. From now on I will go preach to the Gentiles" (Acts 18:5-6, NLT).

The word *oppose* in Acts 18 is the same word used as *resist* in James 4. Notice the crowd exhibited hostile, aggressive behavior against Paul. This is the meaning many of us think about when the concept of resisting the devil comes to mind. We think of aggressive behavior toward him. We often think about warring in prayer, binding and losing, and using our authority over the devil in an aggressive way.

No doubt, aggressive resistance is a marvelously effective truth and a principle we need to exercise in our lives. But there are also times when we cannot stop in the middle of what we're doing or where we are to rebuke the devil. Then what?

On multiple occasions, I would be sitting in a church service and the most hideous, tormenting thoughts would bombard my mind. Like a machine gun firing repeatedly, the harassing thoughts would fire into my mind, trying to distract me from the service or the Bible lesson being taught. At that moment, I couldn't do what I would normally do in my prayer time. I could not just start loudly rebuking the devil in the middle of the church service. If I would have done that, they definitely would have come after me with a straitjacket.

I have been in a company of friends or family members when a bad thought or impure thought would pop into my mind. I couldn't just quote scriptures out loud or blurt out, "I resist you in Jesus' name!" That would be confusing and disorderly, and we know confusion is not from God. So how could I exercise resistance in those situations?

Several years ago, I was sitting in a high-level meeting with the leaders of the organization with which I was affiliated. I was there representing all the churches and ministers in our state. The meeting began at 9 that morning, and by 9 that evening, I was done. The meeting was still going, but I had endured enough. My mind was weary, and my body was tired. Sitting in the same chair for twelve hours with only an occasional break had taken its toll on me.

Without warning, a hateful, accusatory thought flashed through my mind about the minister at the podium. Afterward, I immediately thought, *I like that guy. Where did that thought come from?* Suddenly another horrific thought popped into my mind about the organization

I was representing. Then a thought flashed through my mind that I had not entertained in years, *You need to go back to your room and end your life.*

When that occurred, I immediately stood up and was getting ready to shout, "Satan, I rebuke you! Get out of my mind!" But it dawned on me where I was and how many people were sitting around me. Wouldn't that have been some type of scene if I had aggressively resisted the devil and his thought attacks at full volume? Instead, I quietly sat back down with a smile on my face and gathered my notebook and conference items. I turned to the minister sitting beside me and told him I had endured enough for one day and I was going back to my room.

As I walked past several other friends and colleagues, I either stopped and shook their hands and told them I would see them tomorrow or patted them on the shoulder as I walked by. As I walked out of the conference hall, I started humming the old tune, "There's Power in the Blood of Jesus." By the time I arrived at my room, my mind was refreshed. I had some energy in my step, and most of all, those hideous thoughts had evaporated. To this very day, I have not had another situation occur like that again.

I did not resist the devil aggressively, but I resisted him nonetheless. And he ran away. Satan cannot stand it when he is not the center of attention.

In public, I had to learn the power of passive resistance, which simply means I ignored the tormenting thoughts. I have learned that Satan cannot read my mind. He knows what thoughts he has fired into my mind, but he has no idea if those thoughts have found a place of lodging or a beachhead on which to stand. The only way he knows if his thoughts have hit their target is by my actions and my words.

Another meaning of the word *resist* means "to withstand, set against, to stand firm against." This word carries the meaning of "standing your ground." It doesn't necessarily mean aggressive behavior against something but simply taking a stand and refusing to be moved.[7]

By ignoring tormenting, negative, and doubtful thoughts, we are exercising passive resistance. We are standing our ground and resisting the devil. When fearful or ungodly thoughts try to invade our minds, we resist them by not acting on them, not thinking on them, and not speaking them out.

> Each time we don't pay attention to the devil's attempts to harass us, it disarms him a little more in our lives.

What does God's Word promise will happen when we resist the devil? He will flee. It doesn't say maybe he will flee; it says he *will* flee.

Today, I still have moments when unhealthy and fearful thoughts try to invade my mind. Instead of running to my prayer closet to exercise warfare prayer each time a bad thought comes, I have learned to simply resist the thought by ignoring it. Satan hates rejection. Each time we don't pay attention to the devil's attempts to harass us, it disarms him a little more in our lives.

WEAPON# 2—The Name of Jesus

Since I grew up in church, I had been warned all my life about the sacredness of God's name and the danger of taking the Lord's name in vain (Exodus 20:7). I even grew up understanding the need to end my prayers in the name of Jesus, according to John 16:23-24. Yet my understanding of the value of Jesus' name was still limited.

I always knew it was a special name that deserved honor and respect and commanded authority. But it wasn't until I became a prisoner to fear that I discovered the name of Jesus is much more than a name we should respect. The name of Jesus is also a mighty spiritual weapon we possess.

One particular scene from the visitation when Jesus appeared to me in my den is sealed in my memory. It's the image of the monkey-looking creatures (demons) huddled in the corner. Each time Jesus looked at them, they shook with fear. Their fear was so tangible that I could see the hair on their bodies shaking.

During the visitation, Jesus didn't speak to the demons, He didn't rebuke the demons, and He didn't chase them away. No, Jesus simply looked at them. The demons were powerless in His presence. Jesus' presence—His very look—rendered the demons powerless.

Over the years, I have been asked several times why I thought Jesus didn't say something or do something about the devils harassing me. Honestly, soon after the visitation, I had the same question. When the tormenting and harassing thoughts started again, I was hoping Jesus would reappear and take care of the situation as He had done before. He did not.

It was during another onslaught of condemning and accusing thoughts that I remembered what Jesus said to me that day. After He pulled the banners with the tormenting thoughts out of my head, Jesus pointed to the corner of the room and to the two monkey-like creatures and said, "Eddie, there's your problem!"

Jesus pointedly told me those two demons were my problem. Even standing right next to me, Jesus didn't do anything about them. Why? Because He *already* has defeated them.

So you also are complete through your union with Christ, who is the head over every ruler and authority. When you came to Christ, you were "circumcised," but not by a physical procedure. Christ performed a spiritual circumcision—the cutting away of your sinful nature. For you were buried with Christ when you were baptized. And with him you were raised to new life because you trusted the mighty power of God, who raised Christ from the dead. You were dead because of your sins and because your sinful nature was not yet cut away. Then God made you alive with Christ, for he forgave all our sins. He canceled the record of the charges against us and took it away by nailing it to the cross. In this way, he

> *disarmed the spiritual rulers and authorities.*
> *He shamed them publicly by his victory over*
> *them on the cross* (Colossians 2:10-15, NLT).

Paul said we are "in union" with Christ who is the head or ruler over every ruler and authority. Therefore, since we are in union with Christ, we likewise should rule over demonic authorities. Paul also told us how we received our divine authority. When Jesus died on the cross, He forgave, canceled, and eliminated the charges and accusations against us, which also means He disarmed and rendered powerless the condemnation Satan has used against us.

Jesus shamed the demonic rulers and authorities by His victory on the cross. That's the reason the demons in my visitation were so frightened of Jesus. They recognized the One who defeated them and shamed them. They were scared to even look at Him, so they quickly buried their heads.

In the passage below, let's read a story of Christ's authority over Satan before His death and resurrection. The disciples of Jesus had returned from ministering in the cities and villages and were excited because the devils were subject to them. The disciples were able to cast out devils and help people get free.

> *Then the seventy returned with joy, saying,*
> *"Lord, even the demons are subject to us in*
> *Your name." And He said to them, "I saw*
> *Satan fall like lightning from heaven. Behold,*
> *I give you the authority to trample on serpents*

> *and scorpions, and over all the power of the enemy, and nothing shall by any means hurt you* (Luke 10:17-19).

Look at the first sentence once again to see a key element. Notice the disciples discovered that demons were subject to them when they used the name of Jesus. Demons were not subject to the disciples in and of themselves. The demons obeyed the disciples when they were armed with the name of Jesus.

Think about this story. Jesus and Satan were in heaven together. Satan rebelled, and God kicked him out of heaven. Satan came to earth, deceived mankind, and became the god of this world. Jesus showed up on earth, born of a woman.

> The name of Jesus is all powerful in both worlds—heaven and earth.

The authority exercised in heaven over Satan remained in effect when the name of Jesus was used on earth. The name of Jesus is all powerful in both worlds—heaven and earth. That makes Satan a two-time loser in both worlds—heaven and earth.

Peter and John Possess the Name of Jesus

Peter's life and ministry contrasted each other at various times to say the least. He was always talking big and brave in a small company of friends or when he was in the presence of Jesus. But when he was confronted and threatened by the Romans who captured Jesus, his courage left.

*On the way, Jesus told them, "Tonight all of
you will desert me. For the Scriptures say, 'God
will strike the Shepherd, and the sheep of the
flock will be scattered.' But after I have been
raised from the dead, I will go ahead of you to
Galilee and meet you there." Peter declared,
"Even if everyone else deserts you, I will never
desert you." Jesus replied, "I tell you the truth,
Peter—this very night, before the rooster crows,
you will deny three times that you even know
me." "No!" Peter insisted. "Even if I have to
die with you, I will never deny you!" And all
the other disciples vowed the same* (Matthew
26:31-35, NLT).

Jesus told His disciples that He would be betrayed
that night and all His disciples would forsake Him. Peter,
being big, boisterous, and brave, boldly declared that even
if everybody denied Jesus, he would never deny Him. Jesus
responded to Peter and said he would deny Him three
times in just a few hours before the rooster crowed. Not
knowing when to keep his mouth shut, Peter declared,
"Even if I have to die with you, I will never deny you!" And
all the other disciples vowed the same.

Peter wasn't the only one who said he would never
deny Jesus; each of the disciples joined in the conversation with declarations of boldness, loyalty, and courage.
Unfortunately, their courage quickly vanished as Jesus was
arrested a couple of hours later in Gethsemane and carried

away by guards. The disciples followed from a distance, and the word of Jesus came true concerning Peter.

> *Meanwhile, Peter was sitting outside in the courtyard. A servant girl came over and said to him, "You were one of those with Jesus the Galilean." But Peter denied it in front of everyone. "I don't know what you're talking about," he said. Later, out by the gate, another servant girl noticed him and said to those standing around, "This man was with Jesus of Nazareth." Again Peter denied it, this time with an oath. "I don't even know the man," he said. A little later some of the other bystanders came over to Peter and said, "You must be one of them; we can tell by your Galilean accent." Peter swore, "A curse on me if I'm lying—I don't know the man!" And immediately the rooster crowed. Suddenly, Jesus' words flashed through Peter's mind: "Before the rooster crows, you will deny three times that you even know me." And he went away, weeping bitterly* (Matthew 26:69-75, NLT).

Peter had received revelation about the deity of Jesus that the other disciples hadn't received. He walked on the water with Jesus, witnessed the sick healed and the dead raised to life. Firsthand, Peter saw Jesus perform miracle feedings and calm storms by His words. Yet Peter still denied that he knew Jesus when confronted by a servant girl. The bodacious fisherman walked away broken, realizing that Jesus' words about him had become true.

But Peter's story doesn't end there. A few days later on the day of Pentecost, Peter was gathered along with others waiting because Jesus had taught them about a promise yet to come. Suddenly and without warning, a spiritual deposit—being filled with the Holy Ghost—was made into their lives. As a result, those who waited in the Upper Room began speaking in languages they had never learned. This phenomenon created such a stir that thousands of people rushed to the place where this supernatural event was taking place. As the onlookers mocked and questioned what was happening, Peter, the denier, stood up with boldness and courage and preached about Jesus and the power of the Holy Spirit they had just received.

A few days after the Day of Pentecost, Peter and John went to the temple. This was the same area where Jesus had earlier driven out the money changers and created such a stir. It was the same general area where Peter fled from the servant girl who recognized him as a follower of Jesus. But this time, Peter and John were not fearful, denying, or hiding. The Bible tells us they arrived at the hour of prayer at the exact same time the largest multitude of worshippers was present.

We pick the story up in Acts 3:

Peter and John went to the Temple one afternoon to take part in the three o'clock prayer service. As they approached the Temple, a man lame from birth was being carried in. Each day he was put beside the Temple gate, the one called the Beautiful Gate, so he could beg from the people going into the Temple. When he saw Peter and John about to enter, he asked them for some money (Acts 3:1-3, NLT).

Each time I read this story, I am reminded of a humorous play on words that I heard a preacher share concerning this story. The King James Version says, "Now Peter and John went up together into the temple at the hour of prayer, being the ninth hour. And a certain man lame from his mother's womb was carried, whom they laid daily at the gate of the temple, which is called Beautiful, to ask alms of them that entered into the temple; who seeing Peter and John about to go into the temple asked alms" (Acts 3:1-3).

The country pastor was clipping along preaching his message about the lame man at the gate called Beautiful. Without pause, he said, "Isn't it interesting that the lame man asked for "alms" but got legs instead? Hallelujah! God works in mysterious ways." That is not the correct interpretation of this story, but it's memorable nonetheless.

Picking up again with the story of Peter and John, on their way into the temple, they passed a crippled person who daily was brought to the same place to beg for money. He asked Peter and John for alms or money, and this was their response:

Peter and John looked at him intently, and Peter said, "Look at us!" The lame man looked at them eagerly, expecting some money. But

Peter said, "I don't have any silver or gold for you. But I'll give you what I have. In the name of Jesus Christ, the Nazarene, get up and walk! Then Peter took the lame man by the right hand and helped him up. And as he did, the man's feet and ankles were instantly healed and strengthened. He jumped up, stood on his feet, and began to walk! Then, walking, leaping, and praising God, he went into the Temple with them. All the people saw him walking and heard him praising God (Acts 3:4-9, NLT).

Peter responded to the crippled man, saying they didn't have any money to give him, but what they had, they would gladly give to him. They told him in the name of Jesus Christ to get up and walk. Peter and John were filled with boldness on the day of Pentecost, and they were fully equipped and carried the powerful name of Jesus as their possession.

Over the years, I have heard people try to explain this story away as nonapplicable for us today, saying the reason the man was healed was because Peter and John prayed for him. They argue that Peter and John were apostles, and apostles have supernatural power others do not have. Granted, there are power enduements that apostles more frequently operate in than other offices in the body of Christ, but Peter and John clearly declared it was not their apostleship gifts that healed the man. They also said it was not their holiness or personal power.

Let's continue reading:

*They all rushed out in amazement to Solomon's
Colonnade, where the man was holding tightly
to Peter and John. Peter saw his opportunity
and addressed the crowd. "People of Israel,"
he said, "what is so surprising about this? And
why stare at us as though we had made this
man walk by our own power or godliness?"*
(Acts 3:11-12, NLT).

Peter boldly declared what it was they possessed that
healed the crippled man.

*And His name, through faith in His name,
has made this man strong, whom you see and
know. Yes, the faith which comes through Him
has given him this perfect soundness in the presence of you all* (Acts 3:16).

Peter told the crowd it was the name of Jesus and faith
in the name of Jesus that caused the crippled man, who
had never walked in his life, to be healed and walk. The
healing of the lame man created such an uproar that Peter
and John were arrested and taken to jail. The next day they
appeared before the high priest and others who questioned
them about what power or name they used to bring about
this healing.

*They brought in the two disciples and
demanded, "By what power, or in whose name,
have you done this?" Then Peter, filled with
the Holy Spirit, said to them, "Rulers and*

> *elders of our people, are we being questioned today because we've done a good deed for a crippled man? Do you want to know how he was healed? Let me clearly state to all of you and to all the people of Israel that he was healed by the powerful name of Jesus Christ the Nazarene, the man you crucified but whom God raised from the dead. For Jesus is the one referred to in the Scriptures, where it says, 'The stone that you builders rejected has now become the cornerstone.' There is salvation in no one else! God has given no other name under heaven by which we must be saved"* (Acts 4:7-12, NLT).

Again, before the officials, Peter boldly declared it was the mighty name of Jesus that healed the crippled man. Then Peter expounded further, declaring the name of Jesus is the most powerful name on the earth. There is no other name—not another single name—that carries the authority or power the name of Jesus carries.

After hearing this report and witnessing the crippled man healed, the Jewish leaders were dumbfounded and had no defense. They eventually threatened Peter and John and warned them never again to speak or teach in the name of Jesus. They knew who Jesus was and were instrumental in having Him crucified. Undoubtedly, they had spoken the name of Jesus in their own conversations. But when Peter and John used the name of Jesus, the supernatural took place. Remember what Peter said, "It's the name of Jesus and faith in that name."

Once released, Peter and John returned to the group of believers in Jerusalem and had a prayer meeting where again they voiced their faith in the wonderful and miraculous name of Jesus. They didn't shy away from using the name of Jesus but instead prayed more miracles and healings would occur because of that supernatural name.

> *And now, O Lord, hear their threats, and give us, your servants, great boldness in preaching your word. Stretch out your hand with healing power; may miraculous signs and wonders be done through the name of your holy servant Jesus." After this prayer, the meeting place shook, and they were all filled with the Holy Spirit. Then they preached the word of God with boldness* (Acts 4:29-31, NLT).

It's vitally important we understand that faith in that name also means a reverence and respect for the name of Jesus. We cannot flippantly use the name of Jesus or call that name in vain and then turn around and expect the name to have power when we need it. These few back-to-back stories in the book of Acts reveal that the early church depended upon and believed in the power of the name of Jesus. They also viewed the name of Jesus as their weapon that gave them authority over Satan and sin.

Stop! In the Name of Jesus

A family friend called one day to tell me that her husband was verbally and physically abusing her. Having known this person for years, I asked her if he had ever before exhibited this type of behavior.

She said no and explained that in the past he had gotten mad and said some unkind things, but he had never raised a hand to physically harm her. As she shared that information, I

> We cannot flippantly use the name of Jesus or call that name in vain and then turn around and expect the name to have power when we need it.

realized we were dealing with an evil spirit oppressing her husband. I didn't have time to try and figure out what door he had opened to allow this oppressive spirit into his mind. I just wanted to make sure she was physically safe.

She told me she tried to reason with her husband, prayed for him, begged him to leave, and even threatened to leave him if he didn't stop. Sadly, she really had nowhere to go. She refused to call the police because she didn't want anyone knowing the situation. She felt if he were exposed, he would lose his job and that would send him over the edge. She was afraid he might try to kill her.

We lived a long distance away, so we couldn't get to her quickly to help. I told her to just stay away from him until I could figure out what she needed to do. That night I awoke several times unable to sleep. As I began praying early in the morning, the Lord spoke to me and said, "Tell her to stand in the doorway this afternoon, and as he steps across the threshold, point her finger in his face and loudly and boldly say, 'In the name of Jesus, I command the spirit operating in you to stop and release you.'"

Later that morning, she called me again seeking prayer and counsel. I relayed to her what the Spirit had told me. At first, she explained she was scared to do it—that he would probably mock her and knock her down. But a boldness came over me while talking to her, and I said, "He will be unable to touch you. The name of Jesus is more powerful than the evil spirit operating in him."

After a few more minutes of talking, she said she would do it. After we hung up, all types of fearful thoughts tried to invade my mind. Images of him hitting her or knocking her to the floor tried to create stress and fear in me. A couple of times during the day, I was tempted to call her and tell her not to do it because doubt was trying to steal my faith.

As the time drew closer for him to arrive home, I secluded myself and prayed, taking authority over all evil spirits trying to destroy this husband and our family friend.

The time passed when he normally came home, and I heard nothing. Almost an hour later, my phone rang, and I quickly answered. On the other end, I heard her voice trying to talk to me, but she was crying so hard it was difficult to make out what she was saying. Fear gripped me, and thoughts battered my mind. *You've done it now! It didn't work! He has beat her up!*

"Are you okay? Are you okay?" I yelled into the phone.

After a short pause, she said, "Yes, I am okay." She then composed herself enough to tell me what happened.

She explained that fear tried to get her not to go through with it, but she couldn't live in fear any longer.

"So I met him at the door," she said, "and as he opened the storm door, I stepped in the doorway, pointed my finger toward him, and yelled, 'You evil spirit harassing my husband, leave him now in the name of Jesus!'"

"He froze like a statue and couldn't say anything," she said. "Then a moment later, he fell face first across the doorway, crying, and asking me to forgive him."

Many years have passed since then, and they are still happily married.

The powerful name of Jesus is the possession of the Church today. As we honor, revere, and believe by faith in that name, the name of Jesus will become more than a common name. It will become a powerful weapon that will pull down strongholds in our lives.

WEAPON #3—The Blood of Jesus

The third weapon at our disposal is one often overlooked and misunderstood, yet the power of this formidable weapon dates back to the children of Israel and their deliverance from Egypt. Our third weapon able to pull down strongholds is the precious blood of Jesus.

While exiled on the isle of Patmos for his faith in Christ Jesus, the apostle John received an amazing vision we commonly refer to as the last book of the New Testament, the book of Revelation. During this revelation of Jesus and the end times, John also gains insight about Satan and his tactics. Look with me at the following passage:

Then there was war in heaven. Michael and his angels fought against the dragon and his angels. And the dragon lost the battle, and he and his angels were forced out of heaven. This great dragon—the ancient serpent called the devil, or Satan, the one deceiving the whole world—was thrown down to the earth with all his angels. Then I heard a loud voice shouting across the heavens, "It has come at last—salvation and power and the Kingdom of our God, and the authority of his Christ. For the accuser of our brothers and sisters has been thrown down to earth—the one who accuses them before our God day and night" (Revelation 12:7-10, NLT).

John told the story of a heavenly battle between the archangel of God, Michael, and his angelic associates in a war with Satan, called the dragon, and his demonic helpers. Michael and his angelic helpers prevail in the battle and kick Satan out of heaven. Satan's tactic of deception was revealed, and he was thrown down to earth.

Once the devil fell, an announcement was made across the universe that revealed another of his tactics: condemnation. Notice again the latter part of verse 10, "For the accuser of our brothers and sisters has been thrown down to earth the one who accuses them before our

> I grew up incorrectly thinking condemnation and guilt were tools God used to keep Christians in line.

God day and night" (NLT). The devil's trickery was exposed—he is the accuser of Christians and accuses us continually to God.

One of the reasons Satan was able to easily access my thoughts with the suggestion *You must be demon possessed!* and *God does not love you!* is because I grew up incorrectly thinking condemnation and guilt were tools God used to keep Christians in line.

My friend Terry Law wrote this in *The Power of Praise:*

> Most of us have been taught to think that God is speaking to us when we feel guilty and the devil is lulling us into a spirit of complacency when we feel innocent. We think conviction is God making us miserable. Conviction simply means that God is clearly showing us our sins and admonishing us to change. Sin consciousness has held many Christians in bondage for years. Whenever anyone preached against sin, they say, "that's me." They are constantly aware of the effects of sin in their life. They have never really come into the revelation concerning the realities of the new creation.[8]

If I had not known better, I would have thought Terry lived in my home and attended my little church. I grew up in a theological environment where you were guilty until proven innocent. Although I went to church three or four times a week since birth, I never heard a teaching on our "righteousness" in Christ Jesus. In fact, I didn't know what the word *righteousness* meant until I became an adult.

I spent a lot of time praying as a child and a teenager, not necessarily because I was spiritual, but because I lived with the feeling that God was mad at me and I was displeasing to him. So, when that rogue thought popped into my mind that day, *You must be demon possessed,* I wasn't able to put up a theological fight. In a way, it made sense to me because I was sure God was mad at me.

While the book of Revelation identifies Satan as the accuser of the brethren, the voice from heaven also clearly tells us how Christians can overcome Satan's accusations.

> *And they have defeated him by the blood of the Lamb and by their testimony. And they did not love their lives so much that they were afraid to die* (Revelation 12:11, NLT).

If you have been around the church world very long, you have heard about the blood of Jesus. Yet, many view the blood of Jesus only as a past ingredient of the atonement of Christ with no present-day power on earth. Others only think of the blood of Jesus when they are taking communion, the Eucharist, or the Lord's Supper.

But the voice that sounded from heaven tells us, one and all, that we overcome the accuser called Satan by the blood of the Lamb and by our testimony. Our testimony of what the blood of Jesus has done for us enables us to overcome Satan's condemning accusations.

The Blood of Jesus Redeems and Forgives

In the book of Ephesians, the apostle Paul told us that our redemption was purchased by the blood of Jesus.

> *In Him we have redemption through His blood, the forgiveness of sins, according to the riches of His grace* (Ephesians 1:7).

According to this verse, we have two wonderful benefits because of the blood of Christ. Firstly, we have redemption through His blood. The Greek word used for *redemption* means "to release us from our sin and cancel our debt." The word literally carries the idea of buying us back.

> Our testimony of what the blood of Jesus has done for us enables us to overcome Satan's condemning accusations.

> *And if you call on the Father, who without partiality judges according to each one's work, conduct yourselves throughout the time of your stay here in fear; knowing that you were not redeemed with corruptible things, like silver or gold, from your aimless conduct received by tradition from your fathers, but with the precious blood of Christ, as of a lamb without blemish and without spot* (1 Peter 1:17-19).

The reason the blood of Jesus is so powerful is because it paid the price for our release. Satan no longer has legal hold of the child of God. We have been redeemed or purchased back by the blood of Jesus. The blood of Jesus is not historical symbolism but the invaluable currency that paid the price for our lives for an eternity.

> The blood of Jesus is not historical symbolism but the invaluable currency that paid the price for our lives for an eternity.

The apostle Paul declared the same thing when speaking to pastors:

Therefore take heed to yourselves and to all the flock, among which the Holy Spirit has made you overseers, to shepherd the church of God which He purchased with His own blood (Acts 20:28).

Secondly, we have forgiveness through the blood of Jesus, which Greek scholar Rick Renner addresses in his book *Sparkling Gems from the Greek Volume 2:*

When Paul used the word [*aphiemi* for *forgive*] in Ephesians 1:7 to describe the forgiveness of sins, he was saying that God has permanently dismissed our past sins from us. We are liberated completely from them. He has discharged them from us; He has sent them away; and He has released us from them. The debt we once owed due to past transgressions is canceled and God has freed us from the guilt of those previous actions....[9]

I wish I would have known this truth years ago when Satan was tormenting my mind. The devil daily was reminding me and accusing me of every sin I ever committed. He filled my mind with memories of things from my past that I had not thought about in years. But not anymore, praise God! My testimony—my daily confession and declaration—is I have been redeemed by the precious blood of Jesus. My sins have been sent away from me. When the accuser comes to harass my mind with my past failures and sins, his accusations are rendered ineffective because of what the blood of Jesus accomplished for me.

The Blood of Jesus Is a Shield and Protection

Not only does the blood of Jesus give us a legal right to refute the accusations of Satan, but it also serves as a shield and protection for us. We see the benefits of the blood clearly played out in the Old Testament book of Exodus. The children of Israel were slaves to the Egyptians and cried out to God for deliverance. God sent Moses as the deliverer and instructed him to go to Pharaoh and tell him to let the people go so they could worship their God. But Pharaoh refused, and ten plagues of judgment came upon Egypt.

The tenth plague was the death of the firstborn of every human and creature. Whereas the first nine plagues mainly fell among the Egyptians and the Israelites were spared, the tenth plague was completely impartial and would strike everyone. God told His people there was a way of protection from the tenth plague, but it required *shed blood*.

While the Israelites were still in the land of Egypt, the Lord gave the following instructions to Moses and Aaron: "From now on, this month will be the first month of the year for you. Announce to the whole community of Israel that on the tenth day of this month each family must choose a lamb or a young goat for a sacrifice, one animal for each household. If a family is too small to eat a whole animal, let them share with another family in the neighborhood. Divide the animal according to the size of each family and how much they can eat. The animal you select must be a one-year-old male, either a sheep or a goat, with no defects. Take special care of this chosen animal until the evening of the fourteenth day of this first month. Then the whole assembly of the community of Israel must slaughter their lamb or young goat at twilight. They are to take some of the blood and smear it on the sides and top of the doorframes of the houses where they eat the animal. That same night they must roast the meat over a fire and eat it along with bitter salad greens and bread made without yeast. Do not eat any of the meat raw or boiled in water. The whole animal—including the head, legs, and internal organs—must be roasted over a fire. Do not leave any of it until the next morning. Burn whatever is not eaten before morning. These are your instructions for eating this meal: Be fully dressed, wear your sandals, and carry your walking stick in your hand. Eat the meal with urgency, for this is the Lord's Passover. On that night I will pass through the land of Egypt and strike down every firstborn son and firstborn male animal in the land of Egypt. I will execute judgment against all the gods of Egypt, for I am the Lord! But the blood on your doorposts will serve as a sign, marking the houses where you are staying. When I see the blood, I will pass over you. This plague of death will not touch you when I strike the land of Egypt. This is a day to remember. Each year, from generation to generation, you must celebrate it as a special festival to the Lord. This is a law for all time" (Exodus 12:1-14, NLT).

God told the children of Israel to slay an unblemished lamb and spread the blood on the doorpost. The night the judgment of death came into the land, it would not touch any of those in houses where the blood was on the doorpost. God said, "When I see the blood, I will pass over you." Thus, the feast was given the name *The Passover.* Whoever hid behind the blood was safe. The blood of the lamb was sufficient to save the people from their sins.

Hundreds of years later, as Jesus walked on earth, John the Baptist confirmed Jesus by declaring this:

The next day John saw Jesus coming toward him and said, "Look! The Lamb of God who takes away the sin of the world!" (John 1:29, NLT).

Then Paul wrote to the Corinthians and called Jesus Christ the Passover Lamb:

Christ, our Passover Lamb, has been sacrificed for us (1 Corinthians 5:7, NLT).

Growing up in our little Pentecostal church, I remember the saints often would say, "I plead the blood. I plead the blood over my family. I plead the blood over my life." For years I didn't know what that phrase meant, but today I have learned the value of pleading the blood.

I cannot say it any better than Kenneth W. Hagin said it in his article in the *Word of Faith* magazine titled "I Plead the Blood."

Pleading the blood is not begging God to do something. It is not a statement of unbelief or fear. Pleading the blood activates what happened through the blood of Jesus Christ on the cross. It is asking God to provide what Jesus' blood has already purchased. It's a statement of faith about what happened at Calvary.[10]

Activate what Jesus already purchased for you! Plead the blood of Jesus over your mind! Plead the blood over your thoughts, your life, your family, your home!

The weapons of our warfare are not carnal but mighty through God to the pulling down of strongholds. When addictions, phobias, perversions, and demonic influences invade our lives and minds, we have much stronger weapons to bring them down.

Yet our weapons are useless unless we use them. Our weapons are ineffective unless we fire and launch them. How do we launch them? Through the confession of God's Word, through our praise and prayer, through our release of the power contained in the name of Jesus, and through pleading the blood of Jesus over our lives.

When my mind was being harassed, I combated those tormenting thoughts by speaking God's Word. When the devil bullied my mind, I resisted him. When I prayed, I imagined myself being in union with Jesus, and therefore, I carried the power of His name. When Satan tried to remind me of my past, I remembered and declared my redemption and forgiveness through Jesus' blood.

Encouraged to Overcome

It's also important to understand there were times during my battle that I became weak. The constant mental and emotional struggling has a way of wearing down the most diligent warrior, and I was no exception. There were many days that I felt I couldn't quote another scripture or sing another worship song. There were days when I entertained thoughts of giving up and giving into the torment. On those days, the Holy Spirit was always faithful to send a partner or partners to me help fight the good fight of faith.

People would encourage and remind me of the weapons the Lord has given us all to overcome our enemy.

Over the years, Satan's attacks on my mind haven't had the same effect as they did years ago before I learned how to control my thoughts, but the devil still continues to come back around periodically with worry, moments of anxiety, fear, and even temptation. He picks and chooses his moments. Satan watches, and if we are physically or emotionally weary, he will try to slip something in on us.

The Weapons at Work

Fifteen years after the visitation from the Lord, another situation happened in my life where I needed help getting free. Our church had just built the largest worship facility in the county, and people were attending by the hundreds. I was so naïve that I thought everyone would be excited about a growing church in their city. After all, a church represented good moral values and a place where families were taught how to be a blessing to humanity. Unfortunately, I found out that not everyone views a growing church that way.

A group of citizens were unhappy that their little community had become the growth area of the county. Cars by the hundreds crammed into their community every Sunday and Wednesday. Our church was buying available property around us, for prices above appraised value. We paid more than appraised value so people knew we were being fair to families who had lived in those houses for years. We paid for new city sidewalks and helped with infrastructure improvements. Yet, regardless of what we did, it was not enough.

One day I received a call from the town mayor who invited me to a city council meeting that evening at city hall. Once again, being naïve, I thought they were possibly going to award the church some type of honor or thanks for the all the things we had done for the community. The exact opposite occurred. I walked into an ambush. A group of citizens had formed a militia to run me and the church out of town. They had no demands other than for us to get out. I sat stunned as I was yelled at, falsely accused, and threatened. I apologized that we had apparently inflicted harm on their quality of life, but apologies were not what they wanted. They wanted revenge.

As a sidenote, one of the most hurtful sights of the evening was seeing citizens who were members of other churches in our community in chorus with the insults and accusations being hurled my way. I walked out of that meeting hurt, discouraged, and confused.

On my way home, it was as if Satan jumped on my shoulder and started whispering in my ear: *Yeah, look at you. You have ruined your witness now. The church is supposed to be a blessing, but you have led it to become a curse in this community. You have made enemies you will never win back. The church's reputation is stained forever. You are not the pastor of the largest church in the county who is respected; you are the most hated person in the county. You have embarrassed God and the congregation.*

To be honest, I was not prepared for this attack. We had just concluded a building project that cost over two and a half million dollars. And that was twenty years ago, so you can imagine what it would cost today. I was physically tired and emotionally drained. The church was experiencing rapid numerical growth, which required more staff and systems in place. Unfortunately, I had allowed my prayer life to slip, and I wasn't spending the quality time with the Lord that I needed to spend. I was depleted physically, emotionally, and spiritually, and then the attack came.

> I was depleted physically, emotionally, and spiritually, and then the attack came.

For the next month, the words spoken in that city meeting tormented me day and night. Fear started to grab me again. I knew what was happening, but I couldn't catch up and get ahead of it in prayer. I couldn't pray through the hurt and pain. People from the community would stop by the church during the week to complain about something we were doing. The city manager was calling me multiple times during the week with complaints from neighbors. The militia even started writing letters to the editor of the local paper complaining about me and the church. I was heartbroken and scared. Sleep escaped me, and the vise grip around my head came back. I was scared to go to my church office. I found myself paranoid, thinking everyone was out to get me.

Within two months, the fear had consumed me. I couldn't escape it, and I couldn't logically reason a way out of this ordeal. I tried to talk Amanda into relocating somewhere else and leaving the church. The words of those people harassed me day and night.

Daily thoughts invaded my mind: *You are a failure. Yes, you beat this thing years ago, but this time you have messed up bad. You're done with. Your ministry is over in this community, and this debacle will follow you everywhere you go. What a failure you are.*

During a monthly church board meeting, I finally took off my mask and revealed to the elders my fear, hurt, and pain. I wept like a baby, exposing my vulnerability to them. I had no idea what they would do with their pastor having a nervous breakdown. Would they remove me, ridicule me, blame me, or send me away for treatment? I did not know. I just knew that I was miserable and scared to death.

In unison they rose from their chairs and gathered around, laid hands on me, and started praying. At first, nothing seemed to change. I still felt the pressure around my head, and the fear gave way to embarrassment that I, the pastor, needed prayer. After a few moments, they started to pray in the Spirit, declaring the name of Jesus and the blood of Jesus over my life and my mind. I heard them individually praying scriptures over me, proclaiming God's promises of protection and peace of mind.

In the midst of their praying, I heard a rubber band pop. At the same moment, the pressure around my head instantly left! Peace returned to my mind, and joy overwhelmed me. I felt freer and more refreshed than I had in months. My friends and spiritual partners helped break that stronghold of fear that had tormented me for two months.

Again, the power of 2 Corinthians 10:4 comes to mind, "For the weapons of our warfare are not carnal, but mighty through God to the pulling down of strong holds" (KJV). I experienced once again that every stronghold of Satan begins with a single thought. If you allow the thought to continue, its influence in your life will strengthen with fantasy and an undisciplined imagination. If at that point, you don't demolish those images and fantasies, it will become a stronghold that controls your life, causing you to act in ways you never dreamed of acting.

You see, the problems of life will come to all. It's not a matter of maybe or if—but when. And when problems come, thoughts will come. When they do, what will you do? Will you use your mighty God-given weapons to live in the peace God promises you?

Questions:

1. What are the three major weapons God has given us to defeat the devil and thoughts, strongholds, imaginations, and fantasies that attack our minds?

2. How do you launch and fire these weapons?

3. Can you recall an experience when you used a spiritual weapon to withstand a satanic assault against your mind?

Prayer:

Heavenly Father, I thank You according to Your Word in Revelation 12:10-11 that we overcome Satan by the blood of the lamb and the word of our testimony. I declare with my mouth that I am redeemed by the precious blood of Jesus. The powerful name of Jesus belongs to me, and the Word of God is taking up residence in my heart and mind. Help me daily to remember I am not in this battle without mighty weapons. Teach me, Father, to use my weapons as a highly trained soldier of the Lord. In Jesus' name, amen.

Chapter 9

RENEWING OUR MINDS

AFTER WORKING WITH HURTING PEOPLE FOR MORE THAN FORTY years, I've found one glaring need that transcends age, gender, socioeconomic standing, or cultural background. It is the need to renew our minds with the Word of God.

I will be the first to tell you, that if my mind could have received renewing by someone laying hands on me and praying, I would have flown across the globe or driven thousands of miles to find that person to pray for me. In fact, I did.

Every meeting I had the courage to attend, I would have the speaker, pastor, or evangelist lay hands on me and pray. Often, I received a temporary reprieve from the tormenting thought attacks when people prayed for me, but the reprieve didn't last. The tormenting thoughts always eventually made their way back into my mind.

I was even fortunate enough to have Jesus appear to me in my home and talk to me about my thought life. Jesus revealed to me the one responsible for the hell I was living in mentally, and He set me on a pathway of peace and mental wholeness. But that didn't renew my mind.

Numerous times in our services, Amanda and I will have individuals who are living in mental torment ask us to pray for them that their minds will be renewed. We are happy to pray with them and watch the Holy Spirit saturate them with peace. But, at the same time, we tell each one that our prayers cannot renew their minds. Renewing the mind is not an event but a daily discipline, which we'll discuss in more detail later in this chapter.

Your mind—your pattern of thinking—has been programmed one way for years, and it will take time and discipline to renew your mind with God's Word.

Just think about it. For years we have allowed our minds to watch things, listen to things, meditate, and fantasize about things that often are not pure and godly. We have entertained thoughts and images of lust, gossip, doubt, fear, jealousy, revenge, and dozens of other things that are not Christlike. Then when our thoughts are nearly uncontrollable, we realize that God desires that we be sanctified, set apart for Him, not only spiritually but also mentally in our soulish realm.

> It will take time and discipline to renew your mind with God's Word.

So how do we go about renewing our minds? It will take an understanding of how God made each of us a three-part being and how each part affects the whole. It also requires aligning our thoughts with God's thoughts. There's no question that God wants us walking in peace and freedom in this life, and His Word lays out precisely how to walk in those blessings. So let's examine what the Word says about each part of man and focus on a simple formula to renew the mind.

Pleasing God with a Sanctified Life

The apostle Paul writing to Christians in Rome informs us of something very insightful.

> *I beseech you therefore, brethren, by the mercies of God, that you present your bodies a living sacrifice, holy, acceptable to God, which is your reasonable service. And do not be conformed to this world, but be transformed by the renewing of your mind, that you may prove what is that good and acceptable and perfect will of God* (Romans 12:1-2).

I really like how this same passage reads in the New Living Translation:

> *And so, dear brothers and sisters, I plead with you to give your bodies to God because of all he has done for you. Let them be a living and holy sacrifice—the kind he will find acceptable. This is truly the way to worship him. Don't copy the behavior and customs of this world, but let God transform you into a new person by changing*

*the way you think. Then you will learn to know
God's will for you, which is good and pleasing
and perfect* (Romans 12:1-2, NLT).

In the Romans passage above, Paul wrote to
Christians—not ungodly people—and he gave specific
instructions on disciplines we are to maintain to live a life
pleasing to God.

Let's look at another scripture so we don't take one specific verse and make a doctrine out of it. Paul emphasized
the same theme to believers at Ephesus:

> *if indeed you have heard Him and have been
> taught by Him, as the truth is in Jesus: that
> you put off, concerning your former conduct,
> the old man which grows corrupt according
> to the deceitful lusts, and be renewed in the
> spirit of your mind, and that you put on the
> new man which was created according to God,
> in true righteousness and holiness* (Ephesians
> 4:21-24).

Here the apostle Paul told believers to cease from living
in their old (before Christ) lifestyles and be renewed in
their minds. Once again, I really like how it's written in
the New Living Translation.

> *Since you have heard about Jesus and have
> learned the truth that comes from him, throw
> off your old sinful nature and your former way
> of life, which is corrupted by lust and deception.*

Instead, let the Spirit renew your thoughts and attitudes. Put on your new nature, created to be like God—truly righteous and holy (Ephesians 4:21-24, NLT).

Paul wrote to the believers at Thessalonica and gave them similar instructions:

Now may the God of peace Himself sanctify you completely; and may your whole spirit, soul, and body be preserved blameless at the coming of our Lord Jesus Christ (1 Thessalonians 5:23).

Paul informed the church at Thessalonica that God's highest and best for us is to live holy or sanctified lives. The word *sanctified* in the original New Testament language means "separated." It carries a twofold meaning: *separated from sin* and *separated unto God.*

Over the years, I have talked with numerous people who try to defend their moral goodness as their license for salvation. When I ask them about their relationship with the Lord or where they will spend eternity if they were to die today, a typical response is, "Well, I am just as good morally as those people who attend your church. I don't steal, cheat, or lie, so I am okay with God."

Being a morally good person is a wonderful trait, and sanctification includes good moral behavior. But not committing "popular" sins and being separate from sin altogether do not equal the full definition of sanctification. In other words, just because you are a "good ole boy" does not get your ticket punched to heaven. Your salvation is not dependent on what you do or not do but who is Lord of your life.

Paul also listed in 1 Thessalonians 5:23 the three areas in which God desires us to separate from sin and separate our lives unto Him. Those three areas are *spirit, soul,* and *body.*

> Your salvation is not dependent on what you do or not do but who is Lord of your life.

Daily, I interact with people who years ago accepted Christ as their Lord and Savior. They were born again, and their spirits or hearts were transformed. What happened in their lives is exactly what Jesus declared to Nicodemus.

> *There was a man named Nicodemus, a Jewish religious leader who was a Pharisee. After dark one evening, he came to speak with Jesus. "Rabbi," he said, "we all know that God has sent you to teach us. Your miraculous signs are evidence that God is with you." Jesus replied, "I tell you the truth, unless you are born again, you cannot see the Kingdom of God." "What do you mean?" exclaimed Nicodemus. "How can an old man go back into his mother's womb and be born again?" Jesus replied, "I assure you; no one can enter the Kingdom of God without being born of water and the Spirit. Humans can reproduce only human life, but the Holy Spirit gives birth to spiritual life. So don't be*

surprised when I say, 'You must be born again'"
(John 3:1-7, NLT).

Jesus told Nicodemus that before a person can get into
the kingdom of God, he must have a spiritual rebirth.
Nicodemus was confused and couldn't understand the
concept of going back into a mother's womb to be born
again. To which Jesus said, "Nicodemus, you are thinking
naturally, and I am talking spiritually." Jesus was referring
to a spiritual rebirth, not a natural one.

Paul explained it to the Christians at Corinth like this:

> *Therefore, if anyone is in Christ, he is a new
> creation; old things have passed away; behold,
> all things have become new* (2 Corinthians
> 5:17).

The Living Bible Translation quotes this verse in a
great way:

> *When someone becomes a Christian, he becomes
> a brand-new person inside. He is not the same
> anymore. A new life has begun!* (2 Corinthians
> 5:17, TLB).

When we accept Christ as our Lord and Savior, a spiritual rebirth takes place, and we are born again on the
inside. Our spirits become brand new. That's why we often
see people's desires change once they're born again. They
become new creations; old things pass away, and all things
becomes new. But remember, Paul said God desires for us

to be set apart not only in our spirits at salvation but also set apart in our souls and bodies.

Understanding Man's Three-Part Design

I was fortunate years ago to learn about the three parts of mankind. As one minister so eloquently stated, "You are spirit, you possess a soul, and you live in a body." The real you is your spirit or the person on the inside of you. When you are born again, your spirit man is the one who receives eternal life.

> *For God so loved the world that He gave His only begotten Son, that whoever believes in Him should not perish but have everlasting life* (John 3:16).
>
> *My sheep hear My voice, and I know them, and they follow Me. And I give them eternal life, and they shall never perish; neither shall anyone snatch them out of My hand* (John 10:27-28).

Your spirit man is the one who lives on eternally once your physical man ceases to exist on earth. Paul said something very encouraging about this:

> *I eagerly expect and hope that I will in no way be ashamed, but will have sufficient courage so that now as always Christ will be exalted in my body, whether by life or by death. For to me, to live is Christ and to die is gain. If I am to go on*

*living in the body, this will mean fruitful labor
for me. Yet what shall I choose? I do not know!
I am torn between the two: I desire to depart
and be with Christ, which is better by far; but
it is more necessary for you that I remain in the
body* (Philippians 1:20-24, NIV).

Paul said he was undecided about his future. He said,
"I am torn between the two: I desire to depart...." Depart
from where? He was referring to departing from his body
and going to heaven. He said that would be far better for
him, but it would be better for his friends if he remained
in his body on earth. Who remained in his body? *His
spirit*—the real Paul, the born-again Paul, the Paul who
had eternal life.

Our Physical Bodies

As he continued to outline how man is designed, Paul
explained to the Christians at Corinth that we have spiritual bodies and natural bodies.

*...For just as there are natural bodies, there are
also spiritual bodies* (1 Corinthians 15:44,
NLT).

Our spirits receive new life. They are born again when
we accept Jesus as our Lord and Savior. But our physical
bodies do not get new life. They do not get born again.
Our physical bodies continue to be subject to the pull of
sin and fleshly desires.

Even Paul struggled with the sinful desires in his flesh body:

> *So the trouble is not with the law, for it is spiritual and good. The trouble is with me, for I am all too human, a slave to sin. I don't really understand myself, for I want to do what is right, but I don't do it. Instead, I do what I hate. But if I know that what I am doing is wrong, this shows that I agree that the law is good. So I am not the one doing wrong; it is sin living in me that does it. And I know that nothing good lives in me, that is, in my sinful nature. I want to do what is right, but I can't. I want to do what is good, but I don't. I don't want to do what is wrong, but I do it anyway. But if I do what I don't want to do, I am not really the one doing wrong; it is sin living in me that does it. I have discovered this principle of life—that when I want to do what is right, I inevitably do what is wrong. I love God's law with all my heart. But there is another power within me that is at war with my mind. This power makes me a slave to the sin that is still within me. Oh, what a miserable person I am! Who will free me from this life that is dominated by sin and death?* (Romans 7:14-24, NLT).

Paul was an apostle of God, empowered and used by God to work miracles and heal the sick. He received revelations through dreams and visions and was caught up into heaven and heard and saw things no one else on earth ever experienced. Yet, even Paul, who was born again and mightily used by God, had a flesh problem. How could that be? Paul was born again, but his flesh was not.

Paul became so frustrated with his flesh that he called himself a "wretched man" (Romans 7:24). He also told the Christians in Rome that our physical bodies long for transformation and redemption.

Yet what we suffer now is nothing compared to the glory he will reveal to us later. For all creation is waiting eagerly for that future day when God will reveal who his children really are. Against its will, all creation was subjected to God's curse. But with eager hope, the creation looks forward to the day when it will join God's children in glorious freedom from death and decay. For we know that all creation has been groaning as in the pains of childbirth right up to the present time. And we believers also groan, even though we have the Holy Spirit within us as a foretaste of future glory, for we long for our bodies to be released from sin and suffering. We, too, wait with eager hope for the day when God will give us our full rights as his adopted children, including the new bodies he has promised us (Romans 8:18-23, NLT).

So, this presents a dilemma for us. We are born again, new creations on the inside, indwelled by the Spirit of God. But this new creation is housed and confined in a body plagued with sinfulness and selfish desires. These two forces—the Spirit of God and the pull of sin—war in our lives daily. The strongest force will win the day. Unfortunately, many Christians find themselves behaving in ungodly ways. It's not because they don't love God but because the born-again man on the inside is dominated by carnal, sinful desires in their flesh.

Paul found a workable solution to this challenge, which he told the Corinthian Christians:

> *I discipline my body like an athlete, training it to do what it should. Otherwise, I fear that after preaching to others I myself might be disqualified* (1 Corinthians 9:27, NLT).

The Living Bible translation interprets this verse like this:

> *Like an athlete I punish my body, treating it roughly, training it to do what it should, not what it wants to. Otherwise I fear that after enlisting others for the race, I myself might be declared unfit and ordered to stand aside* (1 Corinthians 9:27, TLB).

Paul informs us that the born-again man on the inside takes control of the flesh man on the outside and tells it what it should do. In other words, Paul refuses to allow his flesh desires to dominate him.

Paul says the same thing to the Christians in Rome:

> *And so, dear brothers, I plead with you to give your bodies to God. Let them be a living sacrifice, holy—the kind he can accept. When you think of what he has done for you, is this too much to ask?* (Romans 12:1, TLB).

Notice he told the Christians to "give their bodies" to God to be living, holy sacrifices. Don't allow your body to be ruled by sinfulness. Take control over your sinful desires and make your body obey your born-again spirit instead of its sinful urges.

> God wants us holy and sanctified in *every way—spirit, soul, and body.*

Look again at this familiar scripture:

> *Now may the God of peace make you holy in every way and may your whole spirit and soul and body be kept blameless until our Lord Jesus Christ comes again* (1 Thessalonians 5:23, NLT).

God wants us holy and sanctified in *every way—spirit, soul, and body.* We understand our spirits are sanctified when we are born again; our bodies are brought under control by yielding them to God and allowing our born-again spirit man to dominate our bodies' sinful urges. But what about our souls?

The Soul of Mankind

One of the most misunderstood parts of mankind is the soul. Often in the church world, we have either combined the soul and the spirit as one, or we have errantly confused the spirit of man as being the soul of man. It's important to understand that the spirit and the soul are two different and distinct parts of man.

Our soul is the part of us that connects with our mind, will, and emotions. It connects with the mental and emotional realm. Our spirit connects with God because God is spirit. And our bodies connect with the natural realm because our bodies are natural.

The soul and spirit of man are so closely connected, it often takes the Word of God to divide and discern between the two.

> *For the word of God is alive and powerful. It is sharper than the sharpest two-edged sword, cutting between soul and spirit* (Hebrews 4:12, NLT).

The greatest need for Christians is for us to get our soulish area—our mind, will, and emotions—renewed with the Word of God.

> *That you put off, concerning your former conduct, the old man which grows corrupt according to the deceitful lusts, and be renewed in the spirit of your mind* (Ephesians 4:22-23).

The word *renew* means "to make new" in the original Greek language. I have often heard the word *renewed* used when explaining how an antique piece of furniture has its finish removed so the furniture can be *renewed* to its original state. Yet, in the Greek, the word *renew* has another facet, which means "to make new but totally different."

The Holy Spirit tells us to renew our way of thinking, making it totally different. In other words, renewing our minds is an intentional action on our part.

I grew up in the Pentecostal tradition, which placed a huge emphasis on apparel and appearance. I was taught that my hair length, my clothing, and the way I looked were a sign of holiness. It was understood that transformation

> Renewing our minds is an intentional action on our part.

from the world was symbolized by one's appearance. But in Paul's writing to the Roman Christians, he told us that transformation from the world is not achieved by appearance at all, but instead by what we think.

> *Do not be conformed to this world, but be transformed by the renewing of your mind* (Romans 12:2).

The word *transformed* comes from the word *metamorpho*, which literally means to "transfigure or transform appearance." To understand this word, think about the metamorphosis that takes place when a caterpillar turns into a butterfly. The caterpillar is slow and slinky and has no flight abilities. In fact, it clings to leaves, tree branches, or something stationary.

The caterpillar—not the most beautiful of species until a drastic change takes place—wraps itself into a sheath known as a cocoon. Four weeks and an amazing process later, the cocoon opens, and a remarkable transformation happens to the caterpillar. It becomes a beautiful butterfly with different traits and appearance than the caterpillar it was before.

Likewise, we become Christians or new creatures in Christ when we are born again. Our hearts or spirits become brand new. But remember we live in a flesh body that is not born again; it continues to desire selfish, sinful things. This is the war between the spirit and the flesh and your heart and your body. The entity that stands between the born-again spirit and the sin urges of the flesh is the soul or mind.

I like to say it this way: It is a simple matter of numbers. Our born-again spirit versus our sin-weakened flesh is one against one. The side that the soul—mind, will, and emotions—sides with will be the direction we will go.

If your mind has been renewed or made new by the Word of God, then it will side with your born-again spirit. Two against one wins every time! You will follow God's plan and purpose for your life. But if your soul or mind has not been renewed with the Word of God, it will side with fleshly desires, and two against one wins every time.

This is why so many Christians who have Jesus living in their hearts fall prey to sinful actions and attitudes.

They allow the unrenewed mind and flesh to override the born-again spirit who wants to follow God. So it's imperative for Christians to get their minds renewed and made new with God's Word.

Imagine a scenario where a born-again person continually renews his or her mind with God's Word. The person memorizes Bible verses and confesses those promises daily over his or her life. At the same time, the person keeps his or her body and its selfish urges under control. When Satan shows up with a temptation or a thought attack, what do you think will happen? That temptation and thought attack will not find a place in that person's life to establish a beachhead or launch an attack.

That's the reason Paul told us to submit our bodies to God, as a holy, living sacrifice and renew our minds to God's Word. A born-again, mind-renewed, body-disciplined individual is impenetrable to Satan's attacks.

A Simple Formula for Renewing Our Minds

As I mentioned earlier, it's critically important to recognize that renewing your mind is not an event but a daily discipline. Not understanding this vital point is the reason many Christians spend their entire Christian lives struggling and falling to temptations caused by mental harassment.

The truth is, too often Christians are unwilling to do the hard work of daily—hour by hour, week in and week out—disciplining their thought lives. Sadly, their unwillingness will cost them their peace of mind.

If your mind—or pattern of thinking—has been programmed the wrong way for years, you will need to renew your mind to think in line with God's Word. It will require time and discipline, but it will be a gateway to God's best for you in every area of life.

Let me share a simple pattern that helped me get my mind renewed. As I was faithful to do these three things, my thinking began to change. It didn't happen overnight, but after several months, I took back control of my thought life. I call this simple pattern "The Three E's."

The Three E's

Evaluate Every Thought

Paul said if you're going to enjoy spiritual victory, you must cast "down arguments and every high thing that exalts itself against the knowledge of God, bringing every thought into captivity to the obedience of Christ" (2 Corinthians 10:5). In other words, you must make an intentional effort to evaluate and review what you think about.

Now, in my own case, I knew my lustful thoughts were sinful and that I shouldn't think those. But I had not considered thoughts of criticism, unforgiveness, slander, self-pity, jealousy, depression, or envy as thoughts I needed to evaluate. I thought that was just a part of life. And it is a part of life—*a defeated life.*

I still remember the day that I received the revelation of this verse, "...take every thought captive"

(2 Corinthians 10:5, ESV). I heard myself say, "My God, how in the world do I do that? It's impossible! I think thousands of thoughts a day. How can I take every one of them captive?"

It was days later when I stumbled upon the statistic I relayed earlier—that the average person thinks 50,000 to 60,000 thoughts a day. At first that didn't help me. How could I take 50,000 thoughts captive? As I continued studying, I discovered that the same average person repeats 90% of those thoughts. So, 45,000 of those thoughts are the same few thoughts.

This is actually good news! If you properly evaluate your thoughts and start taking captive the thoughts that are unhealthy and ungodly, you will soon discover the challenge is not so daunting after all. In reality, there are not that many different thoughts—they're usually the same fearful, lustful, doubtful thoughts over and over.

Let me encourage you to intentionally develop a plan or system to evaluate your thought life. If nothing more, when you find yourself thinking about something that is not God's best, stop yourself. At that moment, say, "Lord, forgive me for entertaining that thought. I take authority over it, and I refuse it access in my mind."

Most of us in the church world have never been challenged to evaluate our thought lives. We are encouraged continually to evaluate our motives and actions, but both of those are simply the product of the thoughts we have been entertaining. It all begins with the "thought life."

If you don't take your thoughts captive, your thoughts will take you captive.

For example, have you ever driven several miles and finally reached your destination only to realize you couldn't remember passing certain places or taking certain turns or streets to get there? Your mind and thought life took you captive on the journey. Your mind was easily swept away by other things, and you were not conscious of what was taking place around your vehicle.

That's why the first step toward renewing your mind is the daily discipline of evaluating your thought life. You will renew your mind one thought at a time!

Eject Unhealthy Thoughts

Once you have discovered a pattern of thinking which is unhealthy, it's important to aggressively eject or remove those patterns from your thought database.

I have counseled wonderful Christians who have a very poor image of themselves. They have developed a pattern of thinking that daily keeps them sad and oppressed because they have entertained thoughts about themselves that are not true. If you think about yourself or view yourself in a manner that disagrees with what God's Word says about you, aggressively eject and kick out those thoughts. Ban them!

I remember walking through my house, repeating over and over, "I am not going to think that way. I refuse to think that way. I will not entertain that thought again because it is not true."

Once you have evaluated a thought pattern in your mind and found it deplorable, you cannot just casually pay it no attention. That thought pattern has established a beachhead and dug into your countenance. You must aggressively uproot it!

Often, we live with these unhealthy and negative thoughts so long that we become comfortable with them. We have learned to survive thinking wrongly. Listen to me! You can survive with wrong thinking, but you will never thrive with wrong thinking. To thrive in life, you must eject bad thoughts and replace them with God's thoughts.

> You can survive with wrong thinking, but you will never thrive with wrong thinking.

Entertain God's Thoughts

Many years later now, I daily repeat to myself what God's Word says about me or whatever situation I am dealing with in life.

The renewing of your mind is a daily discipline that requires you to honestly evaluate the way you think, aggressively eject unhealthy thoughts, and eagerly entertain godly thoughts.

God specifically tells us what thoughts to think about and entertain.

> *Finally, brethren, whatever things are true, whatever things are noble, whatever things are just, whatever things are pure, whatever things are lovely, whatever things are of good*

*report, if there is any virtue and if there is any-
thing praiseworthy—meditate on these things*
(Philippians 4:8).

Though it was many years ago, I still remember my
third-grade class and Mrs. Knapton drilling the multipli-
cation tables into our little brains. We had to memorize
two rows of numbers a week. Week one was the ones and
twos. It didn't take me long to get the ones memorized.
The second week was the threes and fours. Week three we
memorized the fives and sixes. We did that memory exercise until we had worked our way through the number
twelve. Today, all these years later, I remember my multi-
plication tables perfectly. My little mind had the ability to
capture a truth and hold on to it precisely for more than
fifty years.

Likewise, if you will commit Philippians 4:8 to
memory, it will be the guard—the gatekeeper—of your
thought life. Thoughts that try to invade your thinking
but don't meet the standards of Philippians 4:8 will be
recognized and ejected. You then can start entertaining
thoughts that are true, noble, just, pure, lovely, of a good
report, and praiseworthy.

*Summing it all up, friends, I'd say you'll do
best by filling your minds and meditating on
things true, noble, reputable, authentic, com-
pelling, gracious—the best, not the worst; the
beautiful, not the ugly; things to praise, not
things to curse* (Philippians 4:8, MSG).

The Three E's—evaluate, eject, and entertain— changed my life and will change yours also.

Questions:

1. What is the one glaring need for hurting Christians—for every Christian?

2. If you don't take your thoughts captive, what will happen?

3. List the three E's for renewing our minds. What thought have you entertained that you need to use the three E's on?

Prayer:

Heavenly Father, I thank You according to Your word in Romans 12:1-2 that I can renew my mind and change a lifestyle of unhealthy thinking. Help me to discipline my thought life and replace unhealthy thinking with godly and healthy thoughts. Remind me, Holy Spirit, of the importance of a sound and godly mind every day of my life. In Jesus' name, amen.

Chapter 10

What I Didn't Know That Almost Cost Me My Life

Growing up with a family history of mental and emotional challenges, I realized the treatment and perception of mental illness years ago was not as compassionate as it is today. Even public perception was much different. In fact, during my early years in church, I cannot remember hearing a single sermon on mental health or the thought life. I cannot recall a conversation in our home about mental illness, even though there were relatives on my father's side of the family committed to mental asylums. I am sure my parents talked about it among themselves, but it was a subject only spoken of in hushed tones and private conversations.

In all honesty, being a healthy, strong young man, I thought people who dealt with depression or emotional instability were weak and just needed to "suck it up." I didn't understand it and had no sympathy for anyone experiencing those types of challenges. I am sorry to say, in our religious tribe, many attempts to rationalize or explain mental or emotional instability referred to it as demonic possession.

I was comfortable in my beliefs, and on a couple of occasions when I was approached by people struggling with mental problems, I casually told them to "pray through" and "get over it." Today, I look back with regret on those first few years of my pastoral ministry because I was so ill-equipped and unlearned about the reality of mental and emotional disability.

Then it all changed when at the age of twenty-nine "craziness" invaded my life. The remedies I had so flippantly told others to do as a solution—"just suck it up" and "pray through"—didn't work for me. After a few months of constant mental torment, I was bound and experiencing thoughts, images, and feelings I never dreamed I would experience. When I made an appointment with my spiritual leaders for help, I realized they didn't have any more answers than I had. For the first time in my life, I found something that "praying through" would not fix.

Praying through is a Pentecostal term that means you have prayed to the point you know God's answer is on the way, your situation has changed, or you have peace in your heart and mind that everything will be okay.

Today, I still firmly believe in "praying through." There are so many situations the prayer of faith or intercessory prayer will help you get through. But at that time in my life,

I couldn't get through to the place of peace because I lacked knowledge of the thought life and how Satan manipulates our thoughts to keep us in bondage.

Years later, I am thankful that the Holy Spirit has taught me important truths about the soul realm. If I would have known these truths years ago when Satan came with his tormenting onslaught, I would have successfully navigated darkness to victory with the knowledge and power of God.

My lack of knowledge almost cost me my life. So, let me share some simple truths I have learned about the importance of what we think. Not knowing these truths stole peace from my life; I believe knowing them will add peace to yours.

1. Your direction in life is determined by your thought life.

I have learned that we move toward the things we think and dream about. The Word of God makes this very clear.

> *Those who live according to the flesh have their minds set on what the flesh desires; but those who live in accordance with the Spirit have their minds set on what the Spirit desires* (Romans 8:5, NIV).

This verse tells us that if we live according to what our flesh desires, it is because we have our thoughts fixed and consumed on what our flesh desires. On the other hand, if we follow the Spirit's plan for our lives, it is because we have our thoughts fixed on or consumed by what the Spirit desires. This verse specifically lets us know that our mind is the deciding factor on the direction we go in life.

If you can change your thinking, you can change your direction. Your thought life is vital to your destiny!

2. Your quality of life is determined by the thoughts you entertain.

> *The mind governed by the flesh is death, but the mind governed by the Spirit is life and peace* (Romans 8:6, NIV).

The New Living Translation says it this way:

> *So letting your sinful nature control your mind leads to death. But letting the Spirit control your mind leads to life and peace* (Romans 8:6, NLT).

Notice that thoughts governed by flesh desires lead to death. Death represents fruitlessness, emptiness, and barrenness. All of us know people who have lived their entire lives consumed with fleshly desires. That is all they think about, and at the end of the day, their quality of life is empty. But the mind that entertains and maintains thoughts originated by the Holy Spirit is the mind of a person who will enjoy life and peace.

> *You will keep in perfect peace all who trust in you, all whose thoughts are fixed on you!* (Isaiah 26:3, NLT).

Over the years, I've heard well-meaning but ill-informed people make statements like this: "What you think won't hurt you unless you act upon it." But the reality is whatever we continue to think about, we *will eventually act on.*

> Whatever we continue to think about, we *will eventually act on.*

Your thoughts determine the quality of your life—whether you live in peace or death.

3. Satan cannot read your mind. He simply watches your actions and responses to determine his schemes accordingly.

Many people mistakenly believe Satan is an all-powerful, sovereign evil entity who manipulates and controls mankind at will. Nothing could be further from the truth. Remember in the garden of Eden God gave mankind lordship over the earth. God told Adam and Eve to rule and maintain dominion over the earth, the animal kingdom, and the environment.

> *God created human beings in his own image. In the image of God he created them; male and female he created them. Then God blessed them and said, "Be fruitful and multiply. Fill the earth and govern it. Reign over the fish in the sea, the birds in the sky, and all the animals that scurry along the ground." Then God said, "Look! I have given you every seed-bearing*

plant throughout the earth and all the fruit trees for your food. And I have given every green plant as food for all the wild animals, the birds in the sky, and the small animals that scurry along the ground—everything that has life." And that is what happened. Then God looked over all he had made, and he saw that it was very good! (Genesis 1:27-31, NLT).

The only way Satan was able to exercise leverage over the earth and mankind was when Adam and Eve fell prey to deception. Today it is no different. The only leverage the devil has against any of us is through his mastery of deception. We learn in the book of Revelation that Satan's deception is his tool that inflicts the whole world.

> The only leverage the devil has against any of us is through his mastery of deception.

Then I saw an angel coming down from heaven with the key to the bottomless pit and a heavy chain in his hand. He seized the dragon— that old serpent, who is the devil, Satan—and bound him in chains for a thousand years. The angel threw him into the bottomless pit, which he then shut and locked so Satan could not deceive the nations anymore until the thousand years were finished. Afterward he must be released for a little while (Revelation 20:1-3, NLT).

Satan watches your life, and at opportune moments, he introduces a thought of deception that pierces your mind like an arrow. Then he watches to see how you respond. If you take the thought captive and don't act on it by word or action, eventually Satan and his deceptive scheme move on down the road. But if you entertain the thought and start acting and talking according to it, he knows he has infiltrated your life.

4. You are the guardian of your thought life.

As I stated earlier, I was one of many people who believed the inaccuracy that it doesn't matter what we think as long as we don't act on it. But as the Bible teaches us in various places, it does matter what we allow in our minds. It matters a great deal because we will move toward and literally become what we dwell upon.

For as he thinketh in his heart, so is he (Proverbs 23:7, KJV).

The old timers are often ridiculed and accused of spending too much time preaching against things instead of preaching the positive side of every subject. Maybe they periodically went about it the wrong way, but in their hearts, they were trying to prevent a generation from allowing a loose and immoral mindset from captivating our thinking.

We are discovering daily that many of the things they preached against were accurate. Most daily television shows and movies are consumed with sexual implications and crude language. Unfortunately, we have become so accustomed to the lewdness and vulgarity, we don't even give it a thought. Our minds have become seared to an ungodly lifestyle and verbiage. As the old adage goes, "Garbage in, garbage out." In other words, what we take into our minds will eventually come out into our lives.

> Our minds serve as the rudders that turn our lives toward peace or torment.

It is so important that we guard our thought lives with diligence. Our minds serve as the rudders that turn our lives toward peace or torment.

5. You can control your thoughts.

This principle is tough for individuals who have allowed their minds to be undisciplined for years. If you have been lazy with your thought life, the discipline needed to rein in your thoughts will seem nearly impossible. But with exercise and consistent discipline, you *can* bring your thought life under control.

There are many people whose brains fire in an irregular pattern. Things such as trauma, a chemical imbalance, genetic makeup, or self-inflicted causes have brought harm to their physical brains. This creates a situation in which their brain waves do not respond regularly to certain stimuli or situations. Medication is often prescribed to help the physical brain find an equilibrium so the person's thought life can find a proper rhythm and be controlled.

Today we are fortunate to have good medications that help with a person's mental health. Years ago, when I was going through depression and suicidal thoughts, the medical alternatives were limited.

Even today, I still continue practicing "thought discipline." If I hear things that are unhealthy or see something that doesn't contribute to "thought health and wholeness," I immediately remove myself from that influence or turn off what I am listening to or watching. I have learned the hard way that my mind must be protected. Satan wants access to my mind, but I refuse to give it to him.

You can refuse him as well. You *can* control your thoughts. God says you can!

6. You don't have to take ownership of every thought that enters your mind.

When I was going through the darkness in my life, I mistakenly believed every thought in my mind originated from me. So, when a terrible thought surfaced in my mind, I believed I had to be a terrible person because that thought came from me. But every thought we think does not originate from us.

> Every thought we think does not originate from us.

Where do our thoughts come from?

Our brains are amazing machines. We are told that every scene, every word, every smell, every event we have experienced is stored as data in our brains. That's easy to understand because at times we will hear or smell something that takes us back to something in our personal history. The smell or scene happened decades ago, but it has been stored in the mind since that time. Years later, we experience the smell or scene again, and immediately we are transported back to another day and time. Our past experiences create millions of thoughts and memories in our minds.

We've also learned that Satan can introduce thoughts into our minds. God and His Word fill our minds with thoughts. Our environment and culture serve as stimuli for many of our thoughts. Our friends and enemies interject thoughts in our minds. I've also learned that my flesh urges will lead my mind to think certain things. Bottom line, our thoughts come from dozens of places.

So it is important to understand that *you* do not have to take ownership of every thought that comes to your mind. Once this truth became real to me, I saw unwanted thoughts as invaders trying to break in instead of me being a terrible person that God needed to change.

Do you see my mistake? I spent all my time praying about and attacking the wrong thing—myself. Instead, I needed to stand against the real enemy coming against me—the devil and his deceptive reasoning.

7. An unrenewed mind will convince you of a reality that is not true.

There is a famous account in the Old Testament about the children of Israel planning to invade the Promised Land that God said they could have. Moses sent out twelve spies to search out and bring back a report of the land. The spies returned with food from the land, proving the land was as lush and wonderful as God promised. But ten of the spies also brought back a report that caused the people much fear.

> *After exploring the land for forty days, the men returned to Moses, Aaron, and the whole community of Israel at Kadesh in the wilderness of Paran. They reported to the whole community what they had seen and showed them the fruit they had taken from the land. This was their report to Moses: "We entered the land you sent us to explore, and it is indeed a bountiful country—a land flowing with milk and honey. Here is the kind of fruit it produces. But the people living there are powerful, and their towns are large and fortified. We even saw giants there, the descendants of Anak! The Amalekites live in the Negev, and the Hittites, Jebusites, and Amorites live in the hill country. The Canaanites live along the coast of the Mediterranean Sea and along the Jordan Valley." But Caleb tried to quiet the people*

> *as they stood before Moses. "Let's go at once to take the land," he said. "We can certainly conquer it!" But the other men who had explored the land with him disagreed. "We can't go up against them! They are stronger than we are!" So they spread this bad report about the land among the Israelites: "The land we traveled through and explored will devour anyone who goes to live there. All the people we saw were huge. We even saw giants there, the descendants of Anak. Next to them we felt like grasshoppers, and that's what they thought, too!"* (Numbers 13:25-33, NLT).

What happened to the children of Israel is the same thing that happened to me and many people. An unrenewed mind cost them!

Notice what the ten spies reported next:

> *We even saw giants there, the descendants of Anak* [this part is true and accurate]. *Next to them we felt like grasshoppers,* [that is probably true because of their poor self-image] *and that's what they thought, too!"* [completely untrue] (Numbers 13:33, NLT).

The reality is that the people in the land were afraid of the children of Israel, but because the ten spies had an unrenewed mindset, they convinced the entire population of an untrue reality.

Forty years later, Moses was dead, and Joshua had become the leader of Israel. Joshua sent out spies into the same land where Moses had sent spies. These spies connected with Rahab who lived in Jericho, and this is what she says to the spies of Joshua:

> *"I know the Lord has given you this land," she told them. "We are all afraid of you. Everyone in the land is living in terror. For we have heard how the Lord made a dry path for you through the Red Sea when you left Egypt. And we know what you did to Sihon and Og, the two Amorite kings east of the Jordan River, whose people you completely destroyed. No wonder our hearts have melted in fear! No one has the courage to fight after hearing such things. For the Lord your God is the supreme God of the heavens above and the earth below"* (Joshua 2:9-11, NLT).

In essence, Rahab said, "What have you guys been waiting on? We heard about you years ago and what God did for you in Egypt. Our hearts melted when we heard you were coming."

The children of Israel missed out on forty years of blessings because a group of people with unrenewed minds convinced the population of a reality that was not accurate.

On the other hand, every week I spend time trying to convince people of true realities because they have believed inaccurate realities about themselves. In believing a lie, they've missed out on the blessings of God. Sadly, some folks continue to miss out and never receive the blessing.

What will you believe in your life—an inaccurate reality or the truth of God's Word?

Questions:

1. What determines the direction and quality of your life?

2. Does every thought you have originate from you?

3. Are there areas where you are believing inaccurate realities about yourself and your life? What does God's Word say?

Prayer:

Heavenly Father, I thank You according to Your Word in Romans 8:6 that the mind governed by the Spirit is life and peace. I choose to allow my thought life to submit to the Lordship of the Holy Spirit. Help me understand where unhealthy thoughts originate from and refuse to take ownership of thoughts that do not originate from healthy and righteous influences. In Jesus' name, amen.

Chapter 11

FINALLY

HAVE BEEN ASKED MANY TIMES, "WHEN DID YOU GET FREE FROM THE mental torment? Was it a church service or a prayer meeting where you experienced breakthrough? Did someone lay hands on you, or did you experience another vision from the Lord? Was it during a special time of devotion when the anointing of God came upon you in a supernatural way? When did you get free?" To be honest, I don't know when my freedom came. I know that sounds impossible to believe, but it's the truth.

Let me explain. Almost one year after the tormenting ordeal began in my life, I had made some progress and learned some things. I was experiencing moments of peace followed by moments of torment. This was progress for me because for months it was torment every day, all day. So, any respites of peace were a blessing and an answer to prayer.

Finally, I realized one day from reading my Bible that momentary peace of mind was not God's best for my life.

God's highest and best is a mind filled with peace twenty-four hours a day, seven days a week. That's God's highest and best for you, too!

> *You will keep in perfect peace all who trust in you, all whose thoughts are fixed on you!* (Isaiah 26:3, NLT).

> *I am leaving you with a gift—peace of mind and heart. And the peace I give is a gift the world cannot give. So don't be troubled or afraid* (John 14:27, NLT).

> God's highest and best is a mind filled with peace twenty-four hours a day, seven days a week.

Here is the verse that convinced me that permanent peace is a benefit for every child of God:

> *Be anxious for nothing, but in everything by prayer and supplication, with thanksgiving, let your requests be made known to God; and the peace of God, which surpasses all understanding, will guard your hearts and minds through Christ Jesus* (Philippians 4:6-7).

The New Living Translation that I like so well says it this way:

> *Don't worry about anything; instead, pray about everything. Tell God what you need and thank him for all he has done. Then you will experience God's peace, which exceeds anything*

*we can understand. His peace will guard your
hearts and minds as you live in Christ Jesus*
(Philippians 4:6-7, NLT).

Anxiety had dominated my life for a year, causing me
to lose sleep and experience physical sickness. I was full
of anxiety to the point that I had become paranoid and
fearful to leave my house. But as I read these two verses,
I realized it was possible to swap the anxiety I was experiencing with God's peace through prayer and thanksgiving.

I assumed if I increased my personal prayer time that
would enable me to get rid of the anxiety in my life that still
lingered and hung on. Some weeks I had a couple of complete days when I experienced no anxiety. I had moments
when I felt totally free and removed from the hell I had
lived in for the past year, but I couldn't put many of those
days together back to back. Something would happen or I
would hear something that would throw me back into anxiety and fear.

So I decided to increase my prayer time every day. Since
our church was small and my responsibilities were limited, I was able to carve out three to five hours every day to
spend in prayer, and I did. I prayed and prayed and prayed.

After two solid months of praying three to five hours
a day, I stumbled upon something. I realized that the two
verses in Philippians 4:6-7 *actually worked*. It happened
just like Paul said it would. Through prayer and thanksgiving, the peace of God enveloped my mind. As long as
I was praying, peace guarded my mind. It was wonderful!

During those few hours every day, I experienced incredible calm while I soaked in the presence of God.

At the same time, I noticed something I did not understand. The peace of God would come and guard my mind while I was praying, but a couple of hours after I finished praying, anxiety and fear would invade like an unrelenting enemy. As long as I prayed continually and faithfully, the peace was on guard, but when I finished praying, the guard seemed to leave.

It did not take long for me to realize that I could not pray all day every day. I had responsibilities to take care of, a family to help provide for, and church logistics to handle. I know as a pastor I am supposed to pray more than others, but even a pastor has to enjoy a life outside of his prayer closet.

The guard that provided my peace left and went home when I stopped praying, and I needed to find out why. I wondered what I was missing.

It was a Saturday, and I was struggling with anxiety. I told Amanda I was going to spend some time in prayer. She told me I had been praying all week and had even spent a couple of hours praying earlier that morning. She said I needed to spend some time with our son. She was correct, but my mind was running rampant that day. I couldn't settle down my thoughts. I told her again that I needed to spend just an hour praying to calm down my mind, and then I would play with him, to which she reluctantly agreed.

I went to the den, the same den where the Lord Jesus appeared to me. I had not been in there praying for even five minutes when I felt a little hand touching my shoulder. I turned my head to see who was touching me, and there was my little boy who said, "Whatcha doin', Daddy?"

I told him I was praying. His next question has been asked millions of times by children: "Why?"

I hollered at Amanda to come and get Tyler, and she did. I focused my attention back on prayer for a few minutes, and then I heard movement at the doorway opening. I turned to look, and it was my little boy, sitting in the doorway shaking his legs and arms. He saw me looking and smiled at me. I told him to go find Mommy, to which he asked, "Why?"

I tried not to pay him any attention but was unable to, so I got up from kneeling, picked him up, and carried him to his mother who was in the back bedroom. I told Amanda that I was going to pray in the bathroom and to please keep him out. I walked in the hallway bathroom and locked the door. I put the toilet seat down and laid my Bible on the toilet and knelt at the throne. I found a safe place to pray.

I opened my Bible to Philippians 4:6-7 and quoted it aloud, "Be anxious for nothing, but in everything by prayer and supplication, with thanksgiving, let your requests be made known to God; and the peace of God, which surpasses all understanding, will guard your hearts and minds through Christ Jesus."

I remember saying to the Lord, "Lord Jesus, we have a problem. Your Word says if I pray and be thankful, the peace of God will guard my heart and mind. I have found that to be true, but it seems the guard is leaving when I finish praying. I cannot pray twenty hours a day. Lord Jesus, I have other responsibilities to take care of, and I don't know what to do. I know your best is to have peace continually, but the guard who brings peace is leaving when I finish praying."

As soon as that prayer escaped my lips, I heard these words as plain as day on the inside: "Read the next verse."

I recognized that still small voice as the voice of the Holy Spirit, so I looked at the next verse and read it out loud.

Philippians 4:8, "Finally, brethren, whatever things are true, whatever things are noble, whatever things are just, whatever things are pure, whatever things are lovely, whatever things are of good report, if there is any virtue and if there is anything praiseworthy—meditate [think] on these things."

After I read the verse, I said to the Lord, "Yes, that's a good verse. I have read it before, but that doesn't give me an answer. The guard is leaving me. As long as I am praying, the guard brings peace to my mind, but as soon as I finish praying, the peace leaves. So the guard is leaving also, I assume. I can't pray twenty-four hours a day. I have things to do other than pray."

Immediately, I heard these words once again: "Read the next verse."

So for the second time, I read out loud Philippians 4:8, "Finally, brethren, whatever things are true, whatever things are noble, whatever things are just, whatever things are pure, whatever things are lovely, whatever things are of good report, if there is any virtue and if there is anything praiseworthy—meditate on these things."

Again, after I read it, I replied to the Lord, "Yes, Lord, that is a good verse. I have read it many times, but that is not answering my question. Why is the guard leaving? He stays and brings peace as long as I am praying, but as soon as I finish praying, the guard with the peace leaves."

"Read the next verse," I heard yet a third time.

Knowing the voice of the Spirit, I wanted to be obedient, but by now I was getting frustrated. I remember letting out a sigh and starting to read Philippians 4:8 for the third time.

Once again, I read the first word, *"Finally...."* As soon as I read it, it was as if the word lifted off the page in 3D and focused right in front of my eyes. As I knelt there looking at the word *finally*, I heard, "As soon as you finish praying, you have one final thing to do. You are not doing it. That's why the guard is leaving."

Immediately, I read the verse again, and the answer became as plain as day:

> *Finally, brethren, whatever things are true, whatever things are noble, whatever things are just, whatever things are pure, whatever things are lovely, whatever things are of good report, if there is any virtue and if there is anything praiseworthy—meditate* [think] *on these things* (Philippians 4:8).

I saw it.

The reason the peace of God was leaving me was because after I finished praying, I didn't think in line with my praying. After I prayed, I would return to my old way of thinking, and as soon as I did, the guard bringing peace would leave.

Many of you reading this book right now know exactly what I am talking about. You have something troubling you, causing you anxiety and fear, so you pray about it. As you pray, the peace of God comes and gives you a wonderful assurance that everything will be okay. You experience that peace and freedom, and it's fantastic. But after a couple of hours or by the next day, you allow your mind to return to the worry and anxiety. Then before you know it, you need to pray again to regain that peace. As long as you are praying, the peace of God guards your mind, but when you cease praying, the peace leaves because you return to the worry and fear.

> We have one final thing to do after we pray: We must think correctly.

We have one final thing to do after we pray: We must think correctly.

This revelation changed my life. I grabbed a hold of it! I continued to pray for a couple of hours a day, but I refused to entertain thoughts of fear and anxiety during the other twenty-two hours when I wasn't kneeling and praying.

When thoughts of fear and anxiety tried to resurface, I would catch those thoughts, take them captive, and refuse to allow them to wander aimlessly in my mind. Instead, I replaced fearful and anxious thoughts with the promises of God's Word. Exercising this newfound revelation over time, I started experiencing entire days and weeks of perfect peace in my mind.

That's why when people ask me when I got free of mental torment or when my breakthrough actually came, I answer, "I don't know." I walked out this discipline of prayer and thinking in line with Philippians 4:8 following prayer. I purposed to fill my mind with whatever is true, lovely, noble, just and pure, honest, lovely, and of a good report.

I practiced this prayer and thought discipline so long that one day I woke up, sat up in my bed, and shook Amanda from sleep.

"What's wrong?" she asked.

"It's gone!" I said.

"What is gone?"

"The band around my head. The vise grip that had been so tight around my head is gone. The pressure is gone! The anxious, nervous feeling is gone! It's all gone! I am free!"

Amanda hugged me and said, "When did it leave?"

I told her that I didn't know when it left. She asked if it left overnight while we were sleeping. I told her I didn't think so, but it might have. I had been walking by faith for so long, praying and confessing that I was free, that I had completely walked out from under Satan's bondage and didn't even realize when it happened. For we walk by faith, not by sight.

Questions:

1. *Finally*...can you live in peace and take back control of your mind?

2. Does God promise only momentary peace?

3. What is the one final thing you must do after you pray for the guard to stay?

Prayer:

Heavenly Father, I thank You according to your Word in Philippians 4:6-8 that I have a guard who protects my mind from harassment and anxiety. As I pray, the peace of God stands as the guard over my mind, and when I finish praying, a disciplined thought life stands as my guard. Help me daily practice the truths I have learned from Your Word so that I can enjoy peace of mind, a sound mind, and the mind of Christ. In Jesus' name, amen.

Chapter 12

SCRIPTURES TO RENEW YOUR MIND

BELOW ARE SCRIPTURES THAT WILL TAKE THOUGHTS CAPTIVE, TEAR down strongholds, and renew your mind to think like God thinks. Let me encourage you to read them, meditate on them, memorize them, quote them, and allow them to flood your mind with peace.

> *"You will keep in perfect peace all who trust in you, all whose thoughts are fixed on you!"*
> —ISAIAH 26:3 (NLT)

> *"For as he thinks in his heart, so is he...."*
> —PROVERBS 23:7

> *"For though we walk in the flesh, we do not war according to the flesh. For the weapons of our warfare are not carnal but mighty in God*

for pulling down strongholds, casting down arguments and every high thing that exalts itself against the knowledge of God, bringing every thought into captivity to the obedience of Christ."

—2 Corinthians 10:3-5

"Don't worry about anything; instead, pray about everything. Tell God what you need, and thank him for all he has done. Then you will experience God's peace, which exceeds anything we can understand. His peace will guard your hearts and minds as you live in Christ Jesus. And now, dear brothers and sisters, one final thing. Fix your thoughts on what is true, and honorable, and right, and pure, and lovely, and admirable. Think about things that are excellent and worthy of praise."

—Philippians 4:6-8 (NLT)

"For God has not given us a spirit of fear, but of power and of love and of a sound mind."

—2 Timothy 1:7

"Let this mind be in you which was also in Christ Jesus, who, being in the form of God, did not consider it robbery to be equal with God, but made Himself of no reputation, taking the form of a bondservant, and coming in the likeness of men. And being found in appearance as a man, He humbled Himself and became obedient to the point

of death, even the death of the cross. Therefore God also has highly exalted Him and given Him the name which is above every name."

—PHILIPPIANS 2:5-9

"Throw off your old sinful nature and your former way of life, which is corrupted by lust and deception. Instead, let the Spirit renew your thoughts and attitudes. Put on your new nature, created to be like God—truly righteous and holy."

—EPHESIANS 4:22-24 (NLT)

"...Dear brothers and sisters, I plead with you to give your bodies to God because of all he has done for you. Let them be a living and holy sacrifice—the kind he will find acceptable. This is truly the way to worship him. Don't copy the behavior and customs of this world, but let God transform you into a new person by changing the way you think. Then you will learn to know God's will for you, which is good and pleasing and perfect."

—ROMANS 12:1-2 (NLT)

"But people who aren't spiritual can't receive these truths from God's Spirit. It all sounds foolish to them and they can't understand it, for only those who are spiritual can understand what the Spirit means. Those who are spiritual can evaluate all things, but they themselves cannot be evaluated by others. For, "Who can know the Lord's thoughts?

Who knows enough to teach him?" But we understand these things, for we have the mind of Christ."
—1 CORINTHIANS 2:14-16 (NLT)

"Those who are dominated by the sinful nature think about sinful things, but those who are controlled by the Holy Spirit think about things that please the Spirit. So letting your sinful nature control your mind leads to death. But letting the Spirit control your mind leads to life and peace. For the sinful nature is always hostile to God. It never did obey God's laws, and it never will. That's why those who are still under the control of their sinful nature can never please God."
—ROMANS 8:5-8 (NLT)

"May the words of my mouth and the meditation of my heart be pleasing to you, O Lord, my rock and my redeemer."
—PSALM 19:14 (NLT)

"I thought about my ways, and turned my feet to Your testimonies."
—PSALM 119:59

"O Lord, you have examined my heart and know everything about me. You know when I sit down or stand up. You know my thoughts even when I'm far away."
—PSALM 139:1-2 (NLT)

"The Lord knows the thoughts of man, that they are futile."

—PSALM 94:11

"Unless the Lord had helped me, I would soon have settled in the silence of the grave. I cried out, "I am slipping!" but your unfailing love, O Lord, supported me. When doubts filled my mind, your comfort gave me renewed hope and cheer."

—PSALM 94:17-19 (NLT)

"I hate the double-minded, But I love Your law. You are my hiding place and my shield; I hope in your word."

—PSALM 119:113-114

"If any of you lacks wisdom, let him ask of God, who gives to all liberally and without reproach, and it will be given to him. But let him ask in faith, with no doubting, for he who doubts is like a wave of the sea driven and tossed by the wind. For let not that man suppose that he will receive anything from the Lord; he is a double-minded man, unstable in all his ways."

—JAMES 1:5-8

"For out of the heart proceed evil thoughts, murders, adulteries, fornications, thefts, false witness, blasphemies. These are the things which defile a man, but to eat with unwashed hands does not defile a man."

—MATTHEW 15:19-20

"Seek the Lord while He may be found, call upon Him while He is near. Let the wicked forsake his way, and the unrighteous man his thoughts; Let him return to the Lord, and He will have mercy on him; And to our God, for He will abundantly pardon. "For My thoughts are not your thoughts, nor are your ways My ways," says the Lord. "For as the heavens are higher than the earth, so are My ways higher than your ways, and My thoughts than your thoughts."

—Isaiah 55:6-9

"How precious are your thoughts about me, O God. They cannot be numbered! I can't even count them; they outnumber the grains of sand! And when I wake up, you are still with me!"

—Psalm 139:17-18 (NLT)

"Love suffers long and is kind; love does not envy; love does not parade itself, is not puffed up; does not behave rudely, does not seek its own, is not provoked, thinks no evil."

—1 Corinthians 13:4-5

THE FIRST STEP TO CONQUERING YOUR THOUGHT LIFE

THE FIRST STEP TOWARD CONTROLLING YOUR THOUGHTS AND LIVING in the peace God promises is to make sure God Himself lives inside of you. You do this by receiving Jesus Christ as your Lord and Savior, which is the best and most important decision you'll ever make. He will lead and guide you through life and into the blessings that His Word promises you. I invite you to pray this prayer aloud.

> *Heavenly Father:*
> *Your Word says, "Whosoever shall call on the name of the Lord shall be saved" (Acts 2:21, KJV). I call on You right now.*

The Bible also says if I confess with my mouth that Jesus is Lord and believe in my heart that You have raised Him from the dead, I shall be saved (Romans 10:9-10). *I make that choice now.*

Jesus, I believe in You. I believe in my heart and confess with my mouth that You were raised from the dead. I ask You to be my Lord and Savior. Thank You for forgiving me of all my sins. I believe I'm now a new creation in You. Old things have passed away; all things have become new (2 Corinthians 5:17). *In Jesus' name, amen.*

Share Your Good News!

If you prayed this prayer today, please contact our office. We want to hear from you!

Eddie Turner Ministries
P.O. Box 12185
Murfreesboro, TN 37129

ENDNOTES

Chapter 1

1. Hagin, Kenneth E. *What to Do When Faith Seems Weak and Victory Lost*. Broken Arrow, OK: Rhema Bible Church, 1979.

Chapter 2

2. Hagin, Kenneth E. *The Believer's Authority*. Second ed. Tulsa, OK: Faith Library Publications, 1986.

Chapter 4

3. Faith, Hope & Psychology. "80 % Of Thoughts Are Negative...95 % Are Repetitive." Web log. The Miracle Zone (blog), March 2, 2012. https://faithhopeandpsychology.wordpress.com/2012/03/02/80-of-thoughts-are-negative-95-are-repetitive/#comments.

Chapter 5

4. Renner, Rick. "December 1: Fortresses in Your Brain." Entry in *Sparkling Gems from the Greek* Vol. 1: 918-19. Tulsa, OK: Harrison House Publishers, 2003.

Chapter 6

5. Bhandari, Smitha. "Pornography Addiction: Why Pornography Is Addictive?" WebMD. WebMD, March 19, 2019. https://www.webmd.com/sex/porn-addiction-possible.

Chapter 7

6. Law, Terry. *Praise Releases Faith: Transforming Power for Your Life*. Tulsa, OK: Victory House Publishers, 1987.

Chapter 8

7. Vine, W. E., Kohlenberger, J. R., & Swanson, J. A. *The Expanded Vine's Expository Dictionary of New Testament Words*. Minneapolis, MN: Bethany House Publishers, 1984.

8. Law, Terry. *The Power of Praise & Worship*. Shippensburg, PA: Destiny Image Publishers, 2008.

9. Renner, Rick. *Sparkling Gems from the Greek,* Vol. 2. Tulsa, OK: Harrison House Publishers, 2016.

10. Hagin, Kenneth W. "I Plead the Blood!" *The Word of Faith* Vol. LIII, no. 3, April 2020.

ABOUT THE AUTHOR

Pastors Eddie and Amanda Turner have served together in ministry for more than 40 years. Beginning as high school sweethearts, the couple married in 1980 and spent their first three years together pastoring youth in Tennessee. Pastors Eddie and Amanda went on to serve as lead pastors of their first church in Algood, Tennessee, for 20 years, where the congregation grew from 40 to 2,200 in a town of 2,000. The church became the largest in the county. Pastor Eddie served as District Superintendent of the Tennessee Assemblies of God, overseeing 225 churches and 650 ministers for five years. He also served on the Board of Directors of Southeastern University in Lakeland, Florida, for three years and as General Presbyter of the General Council of the Assemblies of God for nine years. After years in executive leadership, the call of the local church pulled on Eddie and Amanda's hearts, and the couple returned to a local pastorate in Murfreesboro, Tennessee. Eleven years later, the church has grown from 350 to more than 1,500. A graduate of Belmont University in Nashville, Tennessee, Pastor Eddie has served on numerous local community boards and organizations and currently sits on the Board of Directors of Fellowship of Ministers International. Currently, Pastor Eddie is the Teaching Pastor at Life Church in Cookeville, Tennessee, and travels extensively coaching pastors and churches. Pastors Eddie and Amanda also travel the world sharing powerful principles to help people live free of mental chaos. The couple are parents to two adult children, Tyler and Cayce, and are proud grandparents as well.

BRANCHES
Recovering Hope • Restoring Lives

The mission of Branches is to be a Christ-centered ministry that facilitates healing and hope for the whole person—mentally, physically, and spiritually.

Services:

- 5-Day Intensive Program
- Life Coaching (Nationwide)
- Individual Counseling
- Weight Loss and Wellness Clinic
- Mental Health Medication Management
- Support Groups

"Our mission has always been to make quality, faith-based counseling accessible to as many people as possible. Our objective is that no client would ever be turned away because of finances."
- Dr. Mike Courtney Ph.D.
Founder and Executive Director

You were designed to be at peace with yourself and others. Let us help you recover hope and restore your life.

How can we help you?

(615) 904-7170

branchescounselingcenter.com

102 Dow St., Murfreesboro, TN

The Harrison House Vision

Proclaiming the truth and the power

of the Gospel of Jesus Christ with excellence.

Challenging Christians

to live victoriously,

grow spiritually,

know God intimately.

Connect with us on

f Facebook @ HarrisonHousePublishers

and **⊙** Instagram @ HarrisonHousePublishing

so you can stay up to date with news

about our books and our authors.

Visit us at **www.harrisonhouse.com**

for a complete product listing as well as

monthly specials for wholesale distribution.